Support and Resistance Simplified

By Michael C. Thomsett

**Foreword by
David S. Nassar, Founder/CEO,
MarketWise Trading School, L.L.C.**

MARKETPLACE BOOKS
Columbia, Maryland

MARKETPLACE BOOKS

Simplified Series

Technical Analysis Simplified
by Clif Droke

Elliott Wave Simplified
by Clif Droke

Moving Averages Simplified
by Clif Droke

Gann Simplified
by Clif Droke

ISBN 1-59280-067-X

Printed in the United States of America.

1 2 3 4 5 6 7 8 9 0

Contents

Chapter 7

Chapter 8

Foreword

I t has been stated that the *simplicity of the market is its greatest disguise.* The concept of "Support and Resistance" (S&R) in the trading markets dates back to the original "Dow Theory," and is perhaps often overlooked today due to its perceived simplicity. The reality is, support and résistance is perhaps the greatest contribution and most widely held concept in technical analysis, and has since become an invaluable method for technical trader and investor alike.

At its most basic level, support and resistance represents the "consensus of value" of all market participants at any given time. With the advent of technology and electronic quote dissemination and execution, newly devised applications make support and resistance an even more robust and far-reaching precept. The progression of S&R's application to market analysis and psychology, when integrated with real-time data derived from today's new software charting programs, has been explosive. As a result, applying support and resistance methods has never been simpler or more effective for trading in today's markets. Conversely, with real-time technology, many participants see support and resistance analysis too microscopically, subjecting them to volatile and choppy whipsaw signals and creating diminished conviction. Therefore, while the concepts have changed little from original Dow Theory, the *application* of the concept in today's market environment has changed significantly. This excellent new primer explains these new dynamics, and the proper use of S&R using modern-day technology.

As the founder and president of the nations most recognized research and education facility for traders, Marketwise Trading School's core curriculum and analysis begins with a thorough understanding of S&R. The integral role "S&R" plays in technical trading is a recurring theme of our classes and seminars and—more importantly—in our own trading methodology. It's absolutely one of the most basic, yet most important, elements of technical analysis, and should be understood by anyone hoping to achieve sustained market success. Why? Because it eliminates most of the "guesswork" and allows you to make logical, well-supported trading decisions—rather than impulsive, emotion-driven decisions.

While Fundamental Analysis answers the question *why* there is movement in the market, Technical Analysis answers the question *when* through the use of chart formations and S&R analysis. Charts are comprised of many forms of market data— including moving averages, patterns, and indicators. This collection of data over time begins to reveal symmetrical patterns of market psychology known as "trendlines." They are primarily represented through the *uptrend* line (the support line), the *downtrend* line (the resistance line), and the channels between them called the *consolidation* and *stabilization* lines. The interplay between these lines, or the forces of supply and demand, form the basis of S&R. By learning to read these patterns and trends across varying time frames, *and* becoming familiar with the psychology that drives them— you gain an edge that can more accurately time your entry and exit points, thereby putting yourself ahead of buyers and sellers to come. And, as savvy investors know, the only way to profit from directional strategies is to buy and sell before others.

Michael Thomsett's *Support and Resistance Simplified* provides an excellent starting point. While not a comprehensive text on technical analysis, it is—by contrast—very accessible. It outlines the primary principles of S&R, furnishes basic applications, and gives you a solid foundation for moving forward to more advanced concepts currently available. For the experienced trader, this book will also serve as a "refresher" for reinforcing good trading habits that are enduring and foundational.

Once you've read *Support and Resistance Simplified* I hope you will be motivated to continue educating yourself on the vast array of technical analysis tools available to today's traders, and continue to sharpen your charting skills. There are many excellent books on technical analysis to help you with this endeavor, including: *Market Evaluation and Analysis for Swing Trading* by myself and Bill Lupien (former Chairman/CEO of Instinet), John Murphy's *Technical Analysis of the Financial Markets,* Thomas Bulkowski's *Encyclopedia of Chart Patterns,* and his new *Trading Classic Chart Patterns,* and the all-time classic *Technical Analysis of*

Stock Trends. There are also courses, workshops and seminars you can attend that will help you refine skills and benefit from the experience of experts—and I encourage you to do so.

As a passionate and dedicated trader, I've learned some hard lessons, and yes painful and costly lessons over the years. But I also know without doubt, the stock market is—and has always been—the single greatest institution to acquire wealth. Every time I took a trading misstep, it strengthened my resolve to develop a way to gain an *edge* in the market. To this day, the simplicity of S&R is the foundation to our successful method of gaining the often-elusive *edge.* We are all students of this dynamic *business* called trading, and because you are reading these words now, you have taken a valuable step toward continuing your education. I congratulate you, and encourage you to continue on this path. Sometimes it's a wild and crazy ride— but it's *definitely* worth it!

Trade Wise!

David S. Nassar
Founder/CEO
MarketWise Trading School, L.L.C.

Introduction

B eating the averages—that is every investor's ultimate goal. Technical analysis is a science that anticipates short-term price changes by using recent patterns, trends, reversals, and ranges. This fascinating topic has as its foundation in the concept of support and resistance, the borders of a trading range in which trading action occurs.

This book explores the important aspects of support and resistance, and shows you how to use the concepts that technicians have developed to improve their own market performance. As the cornerstone of virtually all-technical approaches to price study, support and resistance is perhaps the most important concept you can master in developing your own analytical program. Since it is impossible to consistently and accurately identify the duration of any price trend, we have to depend on support and resistance patterns to look for signals of either change or continuation in price. The support and resistance levels represent a concentration of buying and selling activity. When that concentration begins to evolve, signals develop. The astute technician, recognizing those emerging changes, is then able to act quickly and make buy or sell decisions *before* the market as a whole sees the effects. Once the effects have become obvious, the opportunity to profit has been lost, and that is the essence of the book: by mastering a few basic observations about price patterns as they relate to support and resistance, you will be able to improve your overall timing in the market.

This doesn't mean that you will be able to predict the near-term future—especially concerning stock price movement—even though that idea is compelling. Investors, who assume that the purpose is to reliably predict emerging price trends each and every time, often misunderstand technical analysis, and specifically the various charting tools that it involves. The goal of creating and monitoring charts is not specifically to predict the future; rather, the goal is to improve our forecasting abilities, to better understand the likelihood of the next phase in a pattern.

Market technicians regularly monitor or chart price and volume, and in this process they have developed several specific methods used to analyze and forecast likely price trends and patterns. SR (as we refer to support and resistance throughout this book) has often been equated with the economic forces of supply and demand. However, this is not entirely accurate. Rather, SR acts more as a defining visual representation of price potential versus likely exhaustion levels, a broad range of the current supply and demand factors that are at work on a specific stock. While supply and demand are forces motivating buyers and sellers to interact with one another, SR concentrations—and the trading range itself—define the relative distance between the two levels: the lowest price at which sellers are willing to sell and the highest price at which buyers are willing to buy. From the point of view of technical analysis, in which stock market price is the most important element of study, SR is the defining range, literally the lines of definition. Without the existence of SR range, we have nothing but an unpredictable and random movement of price from one point to another. For example, highly volatile stocks fit that description because price has not settled down into a trading range. By its very definition, "volatility" means rapidly moving, unpredictable, and even random change. No form of analysis—technical or fundamental—can be applied to understand nor to predict the next course of price movement for highly volatile stocks.

With this in mind, the concepts explained in this book can be applied to that vast range of stocks that are trading in a relatively narrow range of price. A very low-volatile stock cannot be submitted to the typical technical tests because it lacks adequate movement and, for that matter, real trend other than the trend of continuing inertia. For any technician, a degree of change is necessary, but not so much that change itself cannot be predicted.

Support and Resistance Simplified offers a thorough overview of how understanding SR functions is an important aid to today's trader. Information is presented in building block fashion, beginning with the basics and introducing in each subsequent chapter the elements of SR that you need in order to master this useful analytical tool. This book illustrates not only the technical elements of SR but also how to apply them to market theories, such as The Dow Theory. Having mastered the various techniques, we conclude with modern day innovations that, while they will not make you right all of the time, you will gain enough of an edge to put you ahead of the averages.

The astute technical analyst recognizes the need to consider and follow a range of potential information. Isolating your analysis only to SR and other charting techniques would only weaken your effectiveness at interpreting information. There are no secrets to anticipating price movement, but there are signals that you can find and use. It is your ability to interpret those signals effectively that will ultimately define the degree of success you experience as a technician and trader. Too many investors are overly focused on charting in isolation and, as a consequence, they overlook the value of other sources of information, including aspects of fundamental analysis and economic or market news. To the degree that other non-technical analysis is included in a comprehensive program, your ability to interpret data will improve. No one system is going to work in every case. The utilization of many types of information cannot provide initial indications of likely market movement; dissimilar information may either confirm what you interpret elsewhere or contradict, and thereby disprove what appears to be an emerging trend.

It is within this concept of confirmation that the real value of analysis is born. By improving your ability to understand the meaning of emerging patterns and signals—and then using independent sources to either confirm or contradict what you have observed—you will vastly improve your own interpretive skills. The use of SR as a foundation for technical observations is an excellent place to start.

While not a thorough primer on every facet of technical analysis itself, this guide gives you the background that all active traders and investors need to make the most timely market moves in today's fast-changing marketplace.

CHAPTER 1

SR: The Foundation of Technical Analysis

The defining nature of SR (Support and Resistance) is what gives it such prominence in the practice of technical analysis. We should remember that the purpose in price analysis is not to accurately predict the future, but to improve our ability to forecast correctly more often than not.

This is where support and resistance play a key role. In studying a chart of recent price movements, we are likely to see a trading range. This is the area of prices that can be clearly identified; recent trading activity is taking place within that range. At the bottom of the trading range is the price (or price trend) known as support. The support price level is an important signal point for identifying likely emerging new trends. This price is where the trend is likely to halt and possibly reverse a down trend—thus the name, "support," which means price support in the current perception of buyers. Support is essentially the lowest price for the stock that is likely to be reached and considered a worthwhile price to pay. If the price of a security has been moving downward, for example dropping from $50 to $25 over recent trading

Trading range: The level of trading in a stock, topped by the price resistance level and bottomed by the price support level.

Support: The lowest price or price trend at which a stock is trading currently in its trading range; the price that buyers currently consider the lowest worthwhile price for that stock.

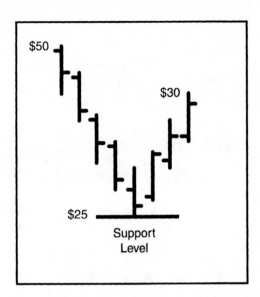

FIGURE 1-1

periods, the price of $25 is the current support level. (Figure 1-1). Resistance serves a similar identifying purpose, but on the top price side of the trading range. A resistance level is the highest price that buyers consider worth paying for the stock. If the stock has been trading between $25 and $30 per share, the $30 level is the current resistance level (Figure 1-2).

Resistance: The highest price or price trend at which a stock is trading currently in its trading range; the price that buyers consider the highest worthwhile price for that stock.

Several writers have treated SR in purely economic terms, equating support with demand and resistance with supply. While this analogy is useful for understanding the market on economic terms, we should also realize that the market forces that go into the creation of price movement often have little to do with economic forces.

In studying fundamental analysis (financial and other recent historical trends of a company), there certainly are economic forces at work. However,

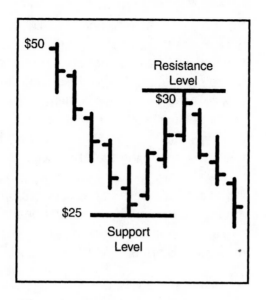

$50

Resistance
Level

$30

$25

Support
Level

FIGURE 1-2

technical indicators have to be distinguished from
the economics of corporations and viewed in terms
of the forces at work in the market itself. When we
think of supply and demand, we usually visualize a
business model. A company creates and markets a
product or service and has to compete with other
companies in the same industry. When there is a
lot of demand for that product, sales rise; when
demand is soft, sales (and profits) fall. In this example, "supply and demand" are factors affecting a
company's profitability.

A study of the stock market reveals entirely different forces at work. Price of stocks really has little to
do with economics as applied to sales and profits,
the traditional models. Rather, prices change due
to investor demand rather than market demand
and the demand itself has nothing to do directly
with a company's competitive success. Of course,

the more profitable companies will have stronger price attributes in its stock, but the forces of supply and demand really do not affect price. In fact, it is fair to say that stock prices rise and fall as a result of a collective market perception of value. Today's rise or fall in a stock's price occurs in anticipation of what will happen next. When investors buy stock, they do so assuming that the price is going to rise; and when they sell, they are taking profits or reacting to changed perceptions about future value. An attempt to tie together the traditional supply and demand features of economics and market price movement is not an accurate approach.

As technical analysts, chartists generally are not at all interested in economic forces such as supply and demand (on a purely market level). Rather, they are interested in the perception of price support and resistance for individual stocks given a number of other factors: current trading range, recent trading patterns within the trading range, whether the range itself has been drifting up or down, signs of support exhaustion, profit-taking, and other trends related to price, not to the economy. SR does not apply well to market indexes, because no one trades the index (except through limited index options). Since an index represents a broad cross-sample of many stocks, it cannot possess an individual SR. While an index trading range may appear to be acting in the same manner as that of an individual stock, it is not the same. The trading range of the index is a culmination of many trading ranges, and it is simply the averaging effect of those components that creates this artificial "trading range."

By the same argument, an index cannot exhibit the patterns known to belong to individual stocks. Since the index is a composite of many stocks, including those with disparate trading ranges and trends, there is a washing effect in the index itself. For many technicians, the index is useless for the purpose of evaluating individual stocks, which is what most investors would be expected to use SR to accomplish.

Even the individual stock will exhibit certain characteristics that may be signals or, in some cases, merely coincidence. We have to assume a certain amount of random movement in the market, if only because the underlying forces are rarely consistent. The interests of sellers and buyers are opposite one another, so no legitimate weight should be given to "the market" as a single entity. In fact, the trading range itself is nothing but the average of market sentiment about that stock. This, however, is where SR is most valuable. We assume that within that overall market for a particular stock, the trading range exists because buyers and sellers have entered into a silent agreement concerning the reasonable price level. Fluctuations occurring within that level, or trading range, represent the day-to-day buying and selling—the jostling among participants—as the price moves around within its trading range. However, the trading range is *not* the range of supply and demand, but rather a reflection of the current status of the auction marketplace. Supply and demand is an economic force that affects prices within markets, and market trading ranges and accompanying SR are the defining qualities inherent in the free

Market trading ranges and accompanying SR are the defining qualities inherent in the free exchange between buyers and sellers.

exchange between buyers and sellers. The distinction is an important one.

Not everyone agrees that there should be such a precise distinction between economic supply and demand versus stock price trends. One author referred to concentrated demand and supply as part of the analysis of why and how prices are likely to move next, and what those trends actually mean in economic terms.[1] The same author observed one general rule of price trends: "supply" (or, more accurately, a new support level) often will be found at a previous trading range's resistance level (Figure 1-3). In other words, when today's trading range is replaced with a new higher trading range, such a shift could be expected to become established. The same is true in the opposite direction: When today's trading range is replaced with a

FIGURE 1-3

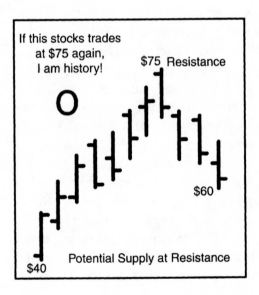

If this stocks trades at $75 again, I am history!

$75 Resistance

O

$60

$40

Potential Supply at Resistance

FIGURE 1-4

new lower trading range, then "demand" (a new resistance level) is likely to be located at or near the previous trading range's support level (Figure 1-4). This is an important concept in the analysis of SR, because as the trading range shifts, we can expect to identify these new support or resistance levels as a starting point for further analysis. However, the debate continues: Do these levels represent supply and demand? Or are they markers for the price levels that provide limits to the auction itself? An observer of market forces will notice that prices seem to move in the most illogical ways, often surprising everyone and defying any logical economic analysis. This alone gives credibility to the belief that SR is a feature of the auction. Were these SR levels truly representative of valid supply and demand forces, then their movement would be expected to occur in some dependable, predictable, and economically sensible manner. In the stock market, this is not a likely manner for prices to move. Instead, the tendency is for the trading range to become established (assuming the stock price is not behaving in an overly volatile manner), which provides a sense of reliability for near-term price movement. In fact, some technical analysts move back and forth between long and short positions based on relative price position within the trading range, based on the presumed dependability of that range in the near term. For such traders, success is most likely when the trading range has been well established in terms of breadth. This means it may be edging upward or downward, but the relative distance between support and resistance remains constant. While trading ranges often broaden or narrow, the most desirable model for a trading range is based on the likelihood that, given interim distortions, the breadth of the trading range is consistent. The longer this consistency lasts, the more stable (and less volatile) price movement is considered to be; and the easier it is for the technician to anticipate price change.

The study of SR usually involves these well-established trading ranges, meaning that, in addition to breadth remaining constant, they unfold over a period of days, weeks or even months. While prices can and do change rapidly within a single trading day, the usual purpose to SR analysis involves current price changes within or away from well-established SR parameters. Trends up or down within a single day may be given many names by chartists, but single-day changes should not be confused with the concept of SR. The usefulness of SR analysis is in providing an established starting

The usefulness of SR analysis is in providing an established starting point to analyze or explain daily fluctuations.

point to analyze or explain daily fluctuations. Thus, any exceptional spikes may be discounted and even ignored as long as they do not become part of a repetitive pattern, testing or violating SR limits. The occasional aberration should be treated as just that and largely ignored.

Some technicians have observed trends in price as "buying and selling waves," noting that such waves can vary in duration, can be exhausted rather quickly, or may be offset by other waves moving in the opposite direction.[2]

This is an important point. A "wave" of short duration might, in fact, serve as a false indicator just like the exceptional spike, misleading the analyst from more dependable, longer-term conclusions. In the study of statistics, such misleading indicators have to be discounted because they do not represent the ongoing trend. They are a reflection of the short-term chaos that is going to characterize any population (individuals, age ranges, political party members, or the random short-term movement of stock prices, for example). The established trading range, with its support and resistance levels, is the more dependable, established trend that is worth observing. By understanding the importance of the range—and also knowing that a breakout (price movement above resistance or below support) does not occur frequently, we are able to stay on course and not be misled by day-to-day aberrations. This is one value to SR; it provides us with a reliable means for evaluating short-term price movement and patterns, ignoring one-time changes and acting only on trends that are confirmed independently (more on these methods later).

Breakout: A price movement above resistance or below support, often the signal that a new trading range is being formed in the stock pricing pattern.

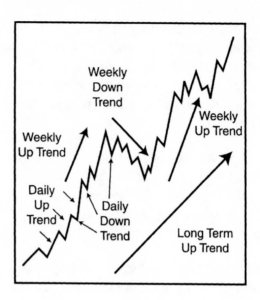

FIGURE 1-5

The long-term trend in a stock's price is the established trading range. It probably is not flat but tends to move gradually in one direction or another, but still with easily distinguished features. Within the overall direction of the long-term trend are weekly trends that are up and down, and within the weekly trends, there are daily trends that are up and down (Figure 1-5). These movements may temporarily violate the established trading range; but without confirming signals, they are not proof of a permanent change. It is the intermediate trend that could forecast an emerging new trend, or one that could become exhausted and disappear. Of even shorter duration, short-term trends last from hours up to days, and finally, the smallest of trends, intra-day trends, last from minutes to hours. Chartists are constantly referring to prices that "test" support or resistance. Thus, a price might move up to resistance and break

SUPPORT AND RESISTANCE SIMPLIFIED

through, only to retreat, or move below support momentarily, but immediately return to the range. A few points to remember about prices "testing" the outside levels of the trading range:

1. Prices are not conscious, so they cannot "test" as a human can. The terminology is misleading in that regard.
2. Short-term trends are entirely unreliable, and in the next chapter, we will examine the two major market theories, both of which agree that short-term trends have to be discounted and even ignored. Chartists know that "tests" are not really forms of reconnaissance on the part of some conscious being but are part of the chaotic nature of price movement itself.
3. The actual price dynamics are not controlled by individuals but as a collective market. The market version of supply and demand is far from the economic form; the auction market-place reflects the interactions between buyers and sellers, all bidding and asking at the same time. Institutional investors (mutual funds, insurance companies, and pension funds, for example) have far more influence on price than the individual or retail investor.
4. You are better off acting within the longer-term price range analysis than reacting to short-term price movement. Such intra-day trends are entirely unreliable for the more studious chartist.

The chartist views SR as the starting point of the chart. Once SR is established, the chartist begins looking for signs of new emerging trends. Three types of charts have come into popular use in

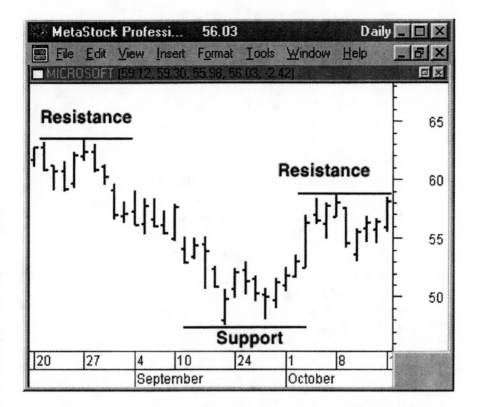

FIGURE 1-6

studying price trends: vertical, figure (today known as point & figure) and wave charts. The vertical charts are the open-high-low-close charts commonly used today (Figure 1-6). Some technicians have not considered chart patterns or technical indicators to be of any value. Instead, they have favored vertical charts for identifying price trend levels, comparative strength and weakness, and from these items the timing of when to buy, sell or place stop orders.[3]

Accumulation area: A price range in which buying activity is taking place, indicating growing support.

Point and figure charts (Figure 1-7) are used to determine accumulation or distribution areas, as well as forecasting price levels that could represent

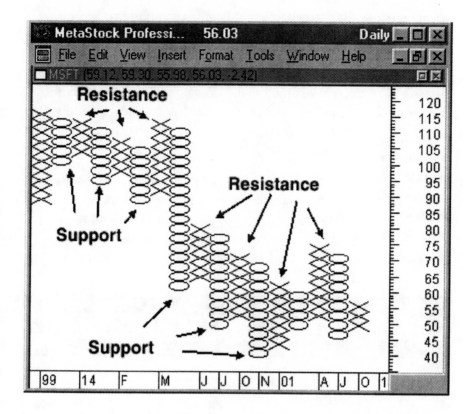

future support or resistance levels. The point and figure chart does not use time for the horizontal axis. Figure 1-7 shows what is called a 3 X 3 chart. If the stock moves up by $3 dollars then an "X" is plotted. As long as there is not a retracement (retreat in the opposite direction) of $3 or more, then the trend is up. If the stock falls by $3, then an "O" is plotted. In Figure 1-7 the downtrend in the middle of the chart is a series of lower support and resistance points.

SR, of course, is not an isolated factor, but the underlying guiding force in chart analysis. Wave

FIGURE 1-7

Distribution area: A price range in which trading is taking place over a longer than average time, in which sellers want to support prices to avoid a decline.

SR, of course, is not an isolated factor, but the underlying guiding force in chart analysis.

Retracement: A movement in prices in the opposite direction from a recent trend.

FIGURE 1-8

charts help identify emerging patterns in SR. Remember, the trading range is rarely unchanging for long. An active stock is likely to trade in a progressing series of trading ranges that gradually move upward and downward, and sometimes reversing course as a matter of trading pattern over time. This is where the wave chart is a useful tool in SR analysis.

Wave charts are line charts (Figure 1-8). They are used to track smaller and shorter-term waves, medium-duration waves, and longer-duration waves. We can measure the duration of each wave, thus identifying the relative strength in what

we perceive to be (a) current trading range and (b) trend direction. For example, Figure 1-8 is a 30-minute line chart of Microsoft, and you can see on the left hand side of the chart how the downtrend from $58 to $48 is a series of falling price points. Notice that during the decline support points give way while resistance levels hold. Next, a double bottom (two tests of the same support level) occurs just above $48, a major warning. Then the resistance level at $52.50 is broken, and now we see rising support points and falling resistance levels.

A cautionary word: Applying the theory of yielding or holding SR levels within single days is contrary to the very idea of longer-term SR significance. The above example is useful for illustrative purposes and momentary changes could serve as dramatic signals as long as they are confirmed independently, and as long as that conclusion is supported in subsequent price changes. However, SR is not useful for making decisions on Intra-day trading. Most day traders are less concerned with SR and are far more interested in price aberrations. Under the SR concept, we prefer to ignore the daily aberrations, recognizing them as just that; and we prefer to use SR as a tool for identifying longer-term trading range trends.

SR is not useful for making decisions on Intra-day trading. The purpose of SR analysis is far more applicable to longer-term analysis.

The purpose of SR analysis is far more applicable to longer-term analysis. Some technicians have observed that accumulation and distribution areas, or trends relating price to volume, are helpful in identifying likely price tops and bottoms.[4]

Under that theory, a downtrend ends when market demand reverses a downtrend. Market supply reverses an uptrend in the same manner. This interaction between demand and supply of securities creates trends and the subsequent reversal of those trends under this theory. Here again, we have to qualify the observation about supply and demand as a matter of definition. It is dangerous to confuse price trends in the auction marketplace with the supply and demand forces at work in the economy. Price of stocks is not directly caused by economic supply and demand. In the context that identifying market tops and bottoms is associated with supply and demand, it is perhaps more accurate to state the theory in another way:

"Observing the accumulation and distribution areas of price in a stock, coupled with observations of changing volume on the buy side or sell side, can be used to confirm the pricing trends that are observed in SR analysis."

We avoid mixing up economic supply and demand in this restated version of the theory to help avoid the confusion. It is a mistake to come to believe that technical analysis and, specifically, charting is a science rooted in economic supply and demand. We can learn a lot, though, from watching how buying and selling activity change along with changes in volume as a means for confirming what we see happening to the stock's trading range.

Interpretation of Price and Volume Together

When buying or selling volume levels change significantly, it could signal a coming change in the price trend as well.

If we limit our observations to price alone, we are likely to miss some important emerging signals. We also need to keep an eye on trading volume. When buying or selling volume levels change significantly,

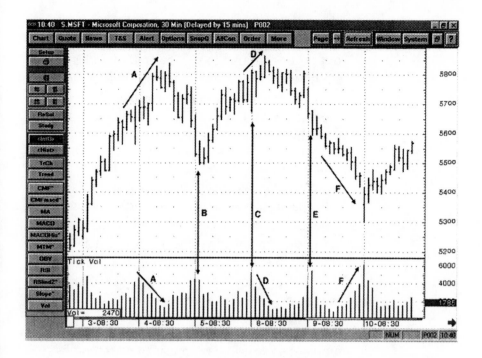

it could signal a coming change in the price trend
as well.

FIGURE 1-9

Figure 1-9 is a 30-minute bar chart of Microsoft
(MSFT). Price trendline A is up but the volume
trendline A is down. As prices have moved higher,
volume has waned, indicting that fewer and fewer
buyers are coming into the market. It appears that
the upward drive is exhausting itself. The price
reacts by retreating back down to form a low at
$55. Here, the volume expanded noticeably,
exhibiting a bottom-heavy activity coupled with a
downside price trend. Bargain hunters step up to
absorb the stock at its softer price level. At point C,
the market opens lower and rallies with volume at
its highest level to this point. But as prices begin to

climb at trend line D, volume recedes. The market rolls over as prices fall; volume expands (Point E) but prices continue to slip lower. Demand is not strong enough to support that price level. Volume continues to rise (trend line F) as price falls, until the price gaps down to $53, and volume reaches its highest point on the chart.

When prices climb and volume falls, buying activity is weakening. As prices fall and volume declines, selling activity is exhausted. As prices fall and volume rises, and as prices then hold in the same area with rising volume, that means buying activity is growing in strength; if prices rise to a point that they stall and volume continues to rise, it indicates that sellers are gaining momentum.

Daily movements of price, as a chaotic and momentary force, may appear to be setting net SR trends but, in fact, are merely part of a larger and longer-term pattern. Of equal importance, remember that identifiable trading ranges are not always present. Highly volatile stocks often have not yet found a trading range, so prices rise or fall in reaction (often overreaction) to many market forces. In those cases of extreme volatility, few charting techniques are of any value. Highly volatile stocks, by definition, do not possess a single trading range and have to be viewed in a larger perspective. A stock's high volatility, in and of itself, makes SR and other charting inapplicable.

Summary

Support and resistance, the study of the interaction between buyers and sellers in relatively low-volatility stocks, is the foundation of technical analysis. As traders, the study of SR gives us a window into how most traders react to price movement. Most traders do not try to forecast short-term price movements, they follow trends as they emerge. The professional or active trader's ability to react swiftly to a new trend helps him to understand the interaction between volume and price. The observant technician understands that SR serves as a starting point for developing an idea of what may occur next in price movements or patterns. However, he also knows that short-term price movement has a random quality to it, and spikes or waves may mislead the impatient trader, causing mistakes and misjudgments. A patient trader awaits confirmation from a suspected change in the current trend, remembering that important change is not going to take place every day. By utilizing other indicators, the technician is able to use SR and emerging chart patterns to anticipate the next step in price trends. The next chapter explains how SR applies to one of the most important theories of the market, the Dow Theory.

The observant technician understands that SR serves as a starting point for developing an idea of what may occur next in price movements or patterns.

NOTES

1 Edwards & Magee, *Technical Analysis of Stock Trends,* Amacon, 1948, 1997

2 Wyckoff, Richard D., *The Richard D. Wyckoff Method of Trading and Investing in Stocks*

3 *Ibid*

4 Gartley, H. M., *Profits in the Stock Market*

CHAPTER 2

The Dow Theory:
Applying SR to Individual Stocks

The application of SR to specific stock price trends has its genesis in many of the theories first suggested by Charles Dow. Among these theories is that of confirmation, the independent signals derived from one indicator that support the same conclusions previously found in another. All technical analysts should recognize the importance of confirmation as they study SR and other chart patterns.

Confirmation: A signal or indicator that supports a previous signal and thus adds to the evidence that a specific technical change is occurring in a price trend.

Formulated by Charles Dow in the late 19th century, what later became known as the "Dow Theory" was originally intended to be used as a forecasting system to anticipate economic conditions, not as a trading system for the stock market. Dow believed that the market was the best prognosticator of the economic future long before the days when such forecasting became dominated by market analysts and fund managers. Dow saw the study of market averages as a viable method for forecasting the direction of the economy. Today, with the Dow Theory used almost exclusively to forecast market-wide trends, there is little economic application other than to use the Dow Jones Industrial Averages (DJIA) to explain other economic changes. However, the DJIA is more often cited today as reacting to economic conditions, rather than anticipating them. So Dow's original theory has been modified to serve different needs, those of the technical analyst. The study of SR as part of the Dow Theory is worthwhile in the sense that these ideas can be applied to individual stocks where they are more useful. Overall market trends are of less interest to the technician, whose time is better spent trying to anticipate price and trend changes in individual stocks.

As a model for studying price movement, the Dow Theory sets down specific "rules" or observations to anticipate future changes.

As a model for studying price movement, the Dow Theory sets down specific "rules" or observations to anticipate future changes. Dow and his partner Edward C. Jones (the two are better known today as "Dow Jones") came up with the idea of using market indexes to track broader trends. Their ideas were published in the financial newspaper that was first printed on July 8, 1889, called *The Wall Street Journal*. (The paper was originally called *Customer's Afternoon Letter* and was in publication since 1882.)

The Dow Theory itself was not formulated until after Dow's death in 1902. Samuel Nelson identified the attributes of the modern theory in his book, *The ABCs of Stock Speculation*.

The Dow Theory originally had one 12-stock market index, later expanded to two; these were based on industrials and transportation stocks (originally called "rails" because only railroad companies were included). These are referred to today as the Dow

Jones Industrial Average and the Dow Jones Transportation Average. A third index, the Dow Jones Utilities Average, was added later on. Dow made extensive use of confirmation. As a basic premise, he determined that in order for a primary trend to exist, both indexes had to confirm the factors required: specifically, in order to call a trend a primary trend, both needed to break through the support or resistance level. If the two averages diverged, that meant the indicator was a false one, because it failed the confirmation test.

Primary trend: The main movement in the market, usually lasting for months or even years, establishing an overall direction for broadly based price trends.

The Dow Theory views the three averages as barometers of likely future market activity. If the market climate is positive (bullish) then trends in prices should be upward. If the mood of the market is pessimistic, that will be reflected in weakening stock prices, and a negative climate (bearish) is likely to pull prices downward. We must remember that, although Dow's original essays discussed the use of market trends to forecast business activity, in modern application it works in the opposite direction: stock price trends among market leaders are used to predict market movement. Thus, weakening economic factors affecting a company's sales and profits are later reflected in lowering stock prices.

To view the components of the three averages or statistical performance summaries, check the Dow Jones website at *http://averages.dowjones.com/jsp.*

The Dow Theory is premised on the idea that trading trends— or overall support and resistance— can be anticipated by way of confirmation.

The averages are studied in search of confirming or contradicting signals. The Dow Theory is premised on the idea that trading trends—or overall support

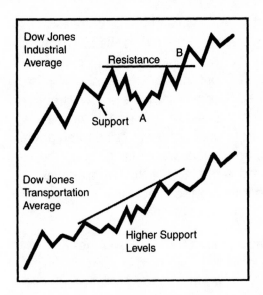

FIGURE 2-1

and resistance—can be anticipated by way of confirmation. Figure 2-1 shows an example of a late confirmation of the trend by the DJIA versus the DJT. At point A the Dow sells off, breaking support levels along the way, but the Transportations continues to trend higher. Then at B, the Dow confirms the up trend again by breaking resistance.

Figure 2-2 is an example of the weekly closing chart for the DJIA and the DJTA for 1997–98. At point A, the DJIA trades down, breaking the previous support points. Next, the DJIA makes a peak followed by a lower peak (trend line C), and closes below support at point D. However, the DJTA diverges by making a new high, but holds support. Next, at point E, both averages are once again in gear, confirming the up trend.

When one average breaks through resistance and the other does not, the "failure to confirm" is a

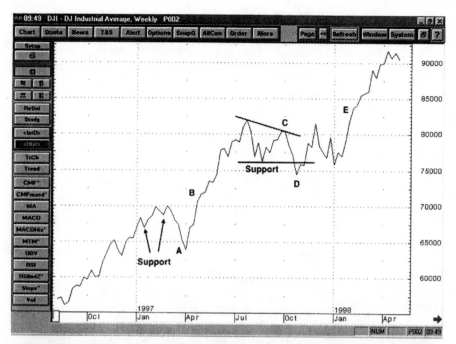

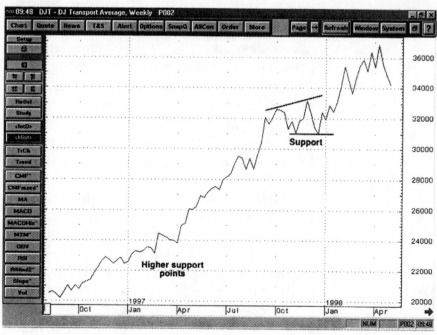

FIGURE 2-2

warning, also called divergence. This should not be construed as a market reversal, but as a trend reversal when both averages break support levels and have falling resistance levels (Figure 2-3).

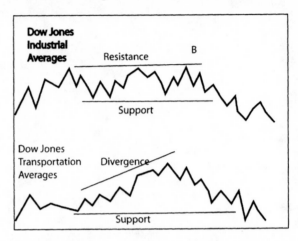

FIGURE 2-3

The divergence between the two averages often precedes confirmation of a newly established down trend. Figure 2-4 illustrates how the divergence indicates trading range price action or a trend reversal. Trend line A is upwards on the Dow, while it is downwards on the Transportations, a typical divergence pattern. Trend line B is up on the Transportations and down for the Dow. Finally, trend line C for the Dow is horizontal, showing strong resistance at 11,250 while trend line C for the Transportations is down. This divergence series ultimately led to a major decline for both indexes. Still, the trading range encompassed approximately two years' trading range activity with multiple divergences before the breakdown occurred. Trading ranges are called lines and can last for a considerable period. During these periods, the astute technician may adopt a more conservative trading approach, as the trend moves sideways until a confirmed new trend begins.

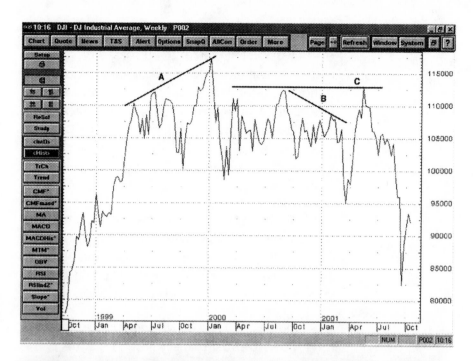

FIGURE 2-4

Elements of the Dow Theory

A study of overall market trends based on market indexes may indicate future *likely* trends; however, using SR in that analysis is not necessarily an accurate exercise. SR is more often used for tracking individual stock prices. Understanding the Dow Theory is useful, however, in viewing how overall market trends may influence prices on specific stocks.

The first observation of the Dow Theory is that **the market tends to follow the leaders.** Thus, an index of 30 industrial stocks, representing about 20% of overall equity value in the United States, is indeed a strong market-wide indicator.[1]

A second belief of the Dow Theory is that **markets have three trends:** primary (lasting months or years), secondary (20 to 60 days) and tertiary (day-to-day).[2]

Trends, which were of great interest to Charles Dow, are what Dow watchers follow, constantly seeking out signals of reversal. After all, just as chartists look for breakouts from SR ranges on individual stocks, **broader market watchers look for three signs when new trends are established**; this is the third belief of the Dow Theory. Those three signs for establishment of a new bull market are:

1. Experienced investors begin buying stocks when market prices are low and the mood is cautionary. This contrarian approach is well known today.
2. Corporate earnings begin to rise.

3. Buying activity in the broader market begins to increase.

A bear market trend would be signaled by these three events:

1. Experienced investors recognize that stocks are over-bought and they begin selling off shares. Even though corporate earnings may be higher than in the past, these investors also know that companies are not going to be able to sustain those growth rates.
2. Buying activity slows down as prices peak out.
3. Market prices decline broadly. Investors rush to sell, creating an accelerating price decline.

These three-step processes are widely recognized, notably by experienced investors whose task is to try and recognize these emerging trends before formal recognition by the market as a whole (and specifically as confirmed under the Dow Theory).

The fourth belief under the Dow Theory is that of confirmation. **Once an average begins to show signs of a reversal in direction, it must be confirmed by the same indication in a second average.** For example, if the industrial averages meet the three tests above, the trend will only be recognized if and when the transportation averages mirror the same steps.

As a final "rule" under the Dow Theory, **a trend is said to remain in effect until *both* averages again reverse direction.** This is the opposite side of belief number four, requiring confirmation of a change in direction.

Market Trends versus Business Trends

The tendency in the market to apply trend analysis against *price* has the result of confusing two separate functions. Price is affected indirectly by corporate earnings, and short-term price is far more a chaotic result of market interactions. Price change in short- and intermediate-term periods should not be given great weight; to truly follow the long-term pricing trends, longer-term moving averages are the only realistic method for following a company's market fortunes.

A business trend, in comparison, is based on fundamentals: sales, costs, expenses and profits. Charles Dow recognized the importance of trend analysis as part of the corporate internal budgeting process, and his original intention was to develop economic models to help anticipate fundamental changes. In modern application, however, the science of trend analysis is applied to overall index trends and to purely technical features, especially to market price. Thus, the concept of applying the Dow Theory to SR is misleading.

To the extent that SR patterns can be anticipated, there are many useful chart patterns and signals and, by using the Dow Theory along with other tools, what appears to be emerging can certainly be confirmed through many outside means. However, SR should be viewed as a separate function of charting—it serves as the basis for technical assumptions, and the Dow Theory is one of many techniques that are used to anticipate price movement. However, remember that there are vast differences between index trends (the net offsetting movements of that index's components) and

To truly follow the long-term pricing trends, longer-term moving averages are the only realistic method for following a company's market fortunes.

individual stock trends, which have isolated and unique price patterns, SR, and other features.

Dow Theory is a useful tool for understanding the nature of moving averages and price patterns. When the concepts employed within the Dow Theory are applied as tools for confirming SR trends in individual stocks, it is quite valuable. However, there is no rational method for applying index trends to individual stocks. SR proponents may gain valuable skills in anticipating stock price patterns using Dow Theory rules, but they should also recognize the built-in limitations when trend analysis, intended as a fundamental tool, is applied in a purely technical environment.

Summary

The Dow Theory is perhaps the best-known of technical theories about the stock market. By understanding how it is applied to indexes of stocks, we can also gain insight into how SR works on individual stocks, at least to a degree.

Just as market-wide forces affect overall bull or bear trends in the market, individual stocks exhibit price swings reflecting ever-changing interaction between buyers and sellers. The trading range identifies the agreed-upon "fair price" area of the stock. Buyers will continue to buy up to the resistance level, but not above; and sellers will be willing to sell down to the support level, but not below. Once prices break out of that trading range, the whole agreement has to be revised. While market-wide changes require confirmation to identify new trends, the same is true

Buyers will continue to buy up to the resistance level, but not above; and sellers will be willing to sell down to the support level, but not below.

for individual stocks. However, breakout signals are given different names. The next chapter identifies how trend lines and channels can be used to spot emerging changes in SR and trading ranges.

NOTES

1 Source: Dow Jones & Company

2 Hamilton, William, in *The Wall Street Journal,* September 17, 1904

CHAPTER 3

Trend Lines and Channels: Techniques to Identifying SR Levels

Trend lines are straight lines drawn on a chart connecting support points for a rising trend or resistance points for a down trend. Figure 3-1 shows a support point using a three-bar pattern where the center bar is the lowest bar. This chart pattern is called a pivot low, isolated low or a three-bar head and shoulders pattern. This pattern is a support point. It represents three attempts by prices to move below support. This pattern occurs frequently at many upturns in the market. The pattern for resistance is called a pivot high, isolated high or three-bar head and shoulders pattern. Downturns in the market often are signaled with one of these patterns.

Support point: A point in a price pattern in which support is tested successfully by prices attempted to break lower.

A trend line may rise, fall or move sideways. Trend lines are not drawn through any price bars; they are used to connect two or more support points that define the trend and indicate its direction (Figure 3-1).

Horizontal trend lines are drawn along the two lowest support points in the trending range. A horizontal trend line is also drawn along two or more

Resistance point: A point in a price pattern in which resistance is tested unsuccessfully by prices attempting to break higher.

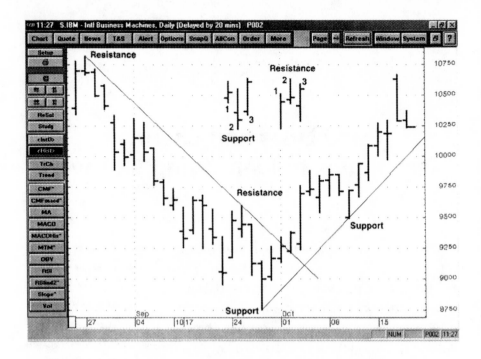

FIGURE 3-1

of the highest resistance points in the trading range. As long as the prices trade between the support trend line and the resistance trend line, the trading range continues (Figure 3-2).

Pivot high or low: The price point at which support or resistance are tested unsuccessfully, after which prices retrace back toward the middle of the trading range.

Two Modern Trend Line Techniques

One expert developed a system for drawing trend lines to clearly define tops and bottoms of the trading range. This technique is referred as the 1-2-3 formation.[1]

First, for a downtrend, the line is plotted along the highs so that the last high shown then becomes the next high preceding the lowest low. A break of this down trend line is step 1 of the formation. This is followed by an upward price movement and

---

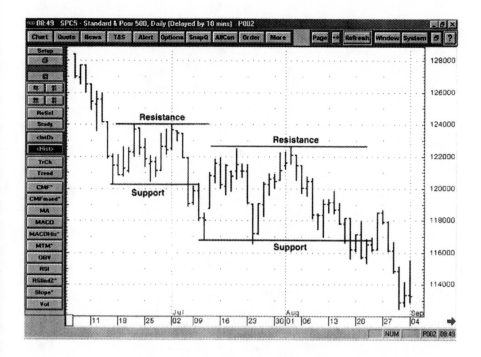

FIGURE 3-2

then a retest of the low. This is step 2. The third and final step is a breakout of the resistance point between the first low and the retest. Figure 3-3 is a weekly chart of Genuine Parts (GPC). The down trend line is plotted across the highs that preceded each new low. At point 1, the down trend line is broken. The market rallies and forms a resistance point. Next, there is a retest of support at point 2. Support holds and the market trades up and breaks through resistance at point 3. A price bottom has been established.

For a top formation the support line has to be drawn along a series of lows that precedes the final high. The first sign of the top is the up trend line is broken. Next, the price pulls back, forms a

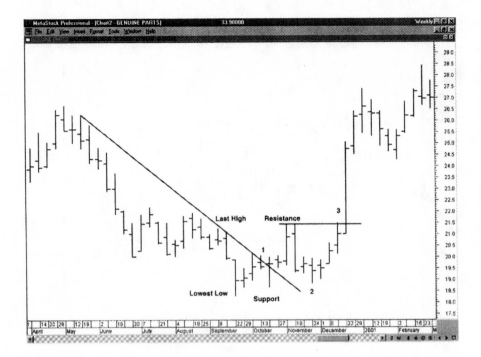

FIGURE 3-3

support point and then retests the high. This is step 2. The third step occurs when prices return back down through support.

Figure 3-4 is a daily chart of the S&P 500 index. The up trend line is drawn along the lows that precede each new high. At point 1, the trend line is broken. The market retraces almost 50% of the decline (point 2). Next, the support level is broken (point 3), and the top formation is complete.

Another method for using trend lines with support and resistance levels is the Andrew's pitchfork or medial line method. Developed by Dr. Alan Andrews, this technique identifies the trend as well as its outer boundaries. The technique identifies three points. For up trends there will be two

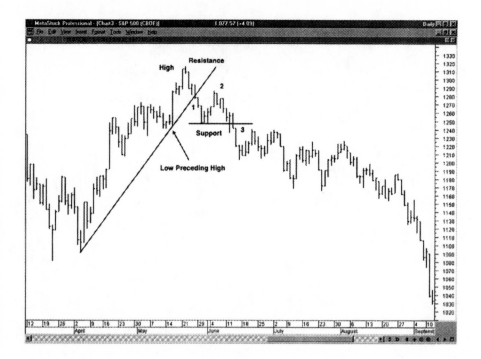

support points and one resistance point, and for
down trends there will be one support point and
two resistance points.

Figure 3-5 has both an up and a down trend using
the Andrew's Medial Line method. For an up trend,
this method first finds the support point (point 1),
the resistance point (point 2) and support point to
the right (point 3). A line connects the high of the
resistance point (point 2) to the low of the second
support point (point 3), and determines the halfway
or median point of this line. Another line is drawn
between the low of the first support point (point 1)
bisecting the median point and extending upward.
One line is also drawn upwards from the resistance
point parallel to the median line, and another

FIGURE 3-4

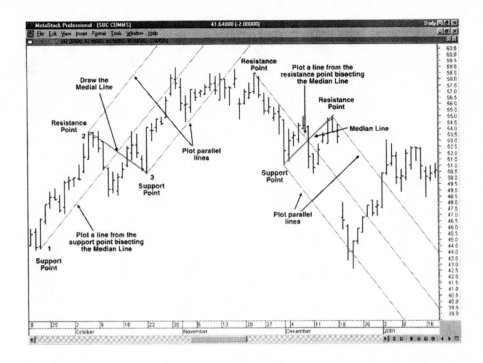

FIGURE 3-5

upwards from the support point parallel to the median line. Technicians use the pitchfork method to identify decision points. For example, they may buy when the median line is pointed upwards and prices have retraced to the support line. Similarly, if the median line is pointed down, they may enter a sell order if and when prices rally back to the resistance line. Penetrations of the support or resistance lines of the Andrews pitchfork may signal that a new trend is underway.

Penetrations of the support or resistance lines of the Andrews pitchfork may signal that a new trend is underway.

Figure 3-5 shows how prices during late October stayed within the lower channel side and only closed above the median line once before prices moved out of the upward channel. Moving below the lower up-channel line signaled an end to the up trend. Next, the market rolled over and new channel pointed downward. When the market gapped down in mid-December, prices reversed at the lower side of the downward channel.

Classic Channels

The up-trend line may also be referred to as the demand line and the resistance points as the over-bought line. The down-trend line plotted over the resistance points may be called the supply lines. A parallel line may be drawn along the lows of the supply lines to identify the oversold area.

Figure 3-6, the weekly chart for the S&P 500, shows a down-trend line along resistance points

FIGURE 3-6

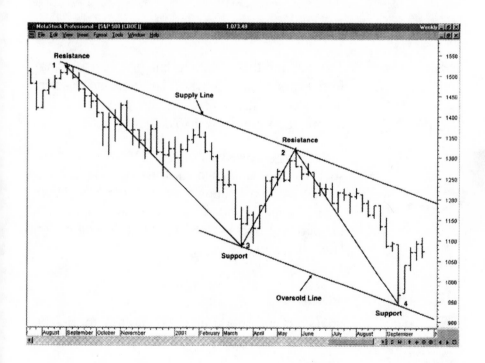

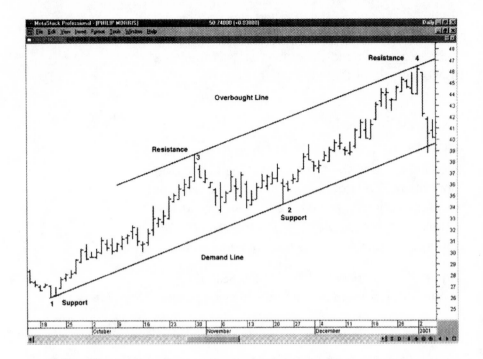

FIGURE 3-7

1 and 2, and then a parallel line (the oversold line) from support point 3, which lies between the two resistance points. Notice how the market rebounded from the oversold line.

Figure 3-7, a daily chart of Phillip Morris (MO), shows an up-trend channel. The demand line is plotted along the support points 1 and 2, and then a parallel line is plotted from the resistance point upward. The prices stopped right at the overbought line in January.

Volume

Volume is an important confirming tool for breaks of trends lines. Figure 3-8, a chart of trading in

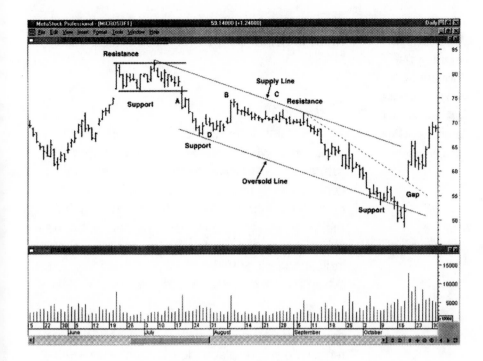

FIGURE 3-8

Microsoft, shows at point A prices breaking down through support. At the same time, volume expands noticeably. Once support is broken it becomes resistance in a newly established trading range. At point B, the market retraced back near the original support level, and volume was heavy, but prices did not return above the original support level. A supply line may be along the two resistance points and the oversold line along the support point D. Prices fell below the oversold line but reversed back into the down-trend channel, accompanied by heavy volume. The next day, the market gapped above the down-trend line (dashed) with heavy volume confirming the breakout. The guideline is to look for an increase in volume to confirm a break of any trend line. In this respect, volume can serve as yet another confirming factor when studying SR—especially when spotting breakouts.

Summary

Trend lines are used to identify support and resistance levels, which may be extended out into the future with a straight line through price and time. Penetration of trends lines may also be accompanied with an increase in volume, further confirming the newly established trend. Light volume breaks of trend lines tend to be false, with that low volume indicating lack of widespread participation or interest on the part of traders and investors.

The next chapter extends trend line analysis to an equally interesting visual study of price. Chart patterns help you to place the trend line into a valuable context.

NOTE

1 Sperandeo, Victor, *Trader Vic—Method of a Wall Street Master*

CHAPTER 4

Chart Patterns: Visual Confirmation of Price Movement

C hart patterns are visual representations of what is taking place in a stock's price movement. Technicians seek out price stability for the purpose of establishing the SR (support and resistance) levels that define trading range. All price patterns can be classified either as *continuation* or *reversal* patterns. A continuation reinforces the existing trend and may be characterized by pausing in price activity, followed by a return to a previous pattern. Reversal patterns provide strong signals that price movement is about to head in an opposite direction, or that an existing trading range is about to be broken and reestablished at a higher or lower level.

In highly volatile stocks, there are no apparent SR levels, because price movement is both erratic and unpredictable. It is *erratic* because there is no trading range to speak of; and it is *unpredictable* because no one knows what is going to happen next. For the chartist, the highly volatile stock is most troubling. As long as there is no SR level, it is

Continuation pattern: A pattern that reinforces the current price trend, including pauses in price movement followed by a resumption of the previous direction.

Reversal pattern: A pattern preceding a change in direction of price movement, or the breaking of a previously established trading range.

also impossible to identify breakout signals, or to make any kind of predictions.

A similar problem exists in low-volatility stocks. If the trading range is well established and movement is generally horizontal, the relatively small price fluctuations provide only one kind of signal: a lack of any change whatsoever. The chartist has nothing to do because no apparent or real change is on the verge of occurring.

In between these two extremes is a rather broad range of stocks, neither entirely volatile nor stable. They are subject to the types of trading range "rules" that make SR analysis interesting; occasional trading ranges keep the chartist actively involved in watching for breakout signals and SR tests; and the trading range itself is dynamic in one direction or the other, or to a degree, moving in alternating waves. This middle range of stocks is far more interesting to the chartist (and to most other analysts) than the extremes. Remember, on the extremes, analysis is either meaningless or impossible, and the chartist can only wait for something to change. However, as long as a stock's activity is dormant or overly volatile, future change cannot be anticipated with any scientific certainty.

An interesting stock exhibits movement. That movement can be studied and quantified using analysis of chart patterns, and changes in trading range and SR can then be made. For example, a stock may over the course of six months move from $45 up to $60, and then trade sideways between $55 and $60. The $55 level would become support and the $60 level would become resistance once price levels off. However, that is a relatively narrow trading range, so the applicable chart pattern should consider the likely effect of the original $45 per share level. That could be considered as initial support, while also recognizing that the trading range has narrowed in more recent sessions. This is a common pattern, but the narrowing is not necessarily permanent. The recent horizontal trading pattern could be merely a short-term price consolidation, meaning that the market is marking time awaiting further news that could propel the price of the stock upwards, or it could be a reversal pattern, signifying the end of the previous up trend and the beginning of a new down trend.

Consolidation: A temporary slowing of price movement and narrowing of trading range, awaiting realignment of buyers and sellers.

The Double Top

The double top shows two price peaks (tests) that are separated by a declining point or range. The initial peak in price often is accompanied by heavy volume, as participants react to bullish news and bid prices higher. The market peaks and retraces a portion of the last move. This pullback will often be accompanied by relatively light volume as the retracement represents profit taking off the high. The price next returns to the original up trend but as it nears the previous peak, buying interest proves not strong enough to push prices to new highs. This inability to break out above resistance is recognized early during the assault on the old high by comparing the volume of the second run to the volume of the first run. If the volume is lighter, it indicates that fewer buyers are joining in on the rally. The signal that indicates when the double top formation is complete comes when prices break down through the support level established between the

Double top: A chart pattern characterized by two price peaks testing resistance, with a decline in between. The unsuccessful test of resistance is viewed as a bearish sign, often anticipating a breakout below previous support levels.

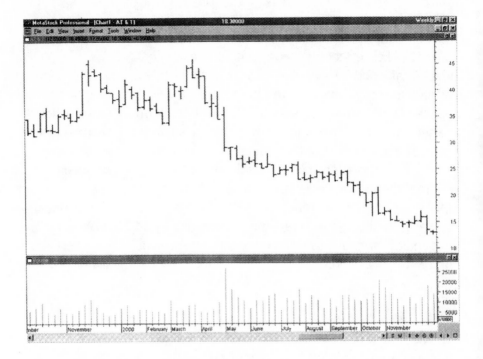

FIGURE 4-1

two peaks. Often, volume will increase dramatically as this occurs, representing the possibility of a major shift in trader expectations.

Figure 4-1, a weekly chart of AT&T, shows a double top with a price break at the support point between the two price peaks. Volume expanded noticeably, confirming the top formation.

Double bottom:
A chart pattern
characterized by
two price drops
testing support,
with a price rise
in between. The

The Double Bottom

The double bottom is characterized by two price troughs that are separated by a price peak. As the price falls to form the first low, volume often is relatively high, at times exceptionally high. However, in the typical double bottom, sellers are unable to break through the support level and a retracement of the decline follows. The price rallies, due to a combination of short covering and bargain hunting. A popular interpretation of the retracement is that the bad news that caused the first price decline is discounted by the point of the second leg, and the market then advances as buyers take up well-priced shares.

unsuccessful test of support is viewed as a bullish sign, often anticipating a breakout above previous resistance levels.

Figure 4-2 shows a double bottom on a weekly chart for American Express. The large volume occurred as the price reached its bottom. A healthy level of support appeared as the double bottom unfolded.

FIGURE 4-2

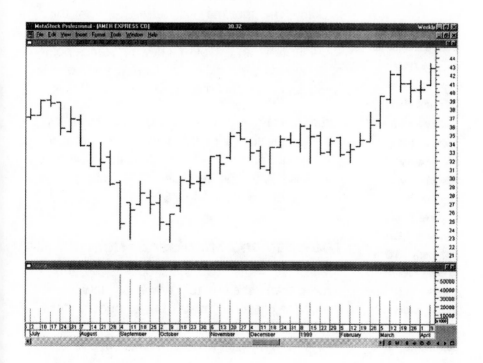

The Head and Shoulders Top

The head and shoulder top is so named for the shape of the chart pattern. It involves a center high level (the head) with lower plateau levels preceding and following (left and right shoulders). Also called an 'M' because of its shape, the head and shoulders is one of the most reliable of all chart patterns. The volume characteristics commonly involve a peak during the left shoulder or at the head, and much lower volume during the right shoulder trading period. The trading area in between each shoulder and the head is often called the neckline. Penetration of the neckline following completion of the pattern signals that the top is complete and a downward price trend is likely to follow. Volume may expand as the price breaks down through the neckline. The price may also retrace and test the neckline in subsequent movements. The head and shoulder top may establish a new resistance point at (or below) the neckline, and a new trading range could become established at or below that level.

Figure 4-3 shows a complex head and shoulders top that developed in IBM. It is complex because the two shoulders show multiple tests of the resistance level. After the neckline at $110 was broken, the price dropped to below $90.

The Head and Shoulder Bottom

The inverse of the head and shoulders top, this pattern marks the end to a previously downward trend. The pattern consists of three price bottom levels with the center (the head) trading lower than the left and right shoulders. A breakout *above* the

Neckline: The trading area in a head and shoulders pattern found between the head and each of the two shoulders.

Head and shoulders pattern: A chart pattern resembling a left and right plateau with a higher center plateau (head and shoulders top) or the reverse (head and shoulders bottom), with a middle lower trading level and higher plateaus trading before and after.

neckline is a sign that a new support level is likely
to be established there as part of a new, higher
trading range. This pattern is also referred to as
'W' due to its distinctive shape.

Figure 4-4 shows that the head and shoulders pattern can represent both a bottom as well as a continuation pattern. The first head and shoulders
bottom occurred in March, then proceeded to rally,
followed by a price decline in April, and finally
another smaller head and shoulders bottom formation. This indicated strong support, and the prices
advanced once again.

As a general observation, the head and shoulders
formation is a strong signal that is either bearish

FIGURE 4-3

**Also called an
'M' because of
its shape, the
head and shoul-
ders is one of
the most reliable
of all chart
patterns.**

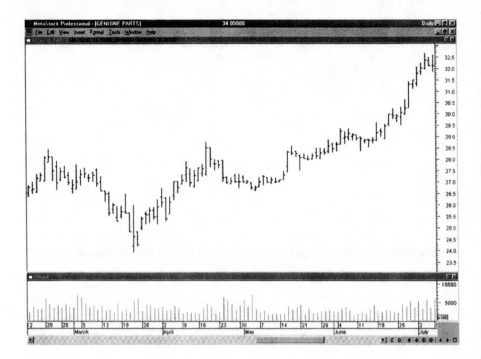

FIGURE 4-4

The importance of head and shoulder formations is in the way that resistance (top pattern) and support (bottom pattern) are tested, and in the forecasting advantage that these patterns provide.

(top pattern) or bullish (bottom pattern). The repeated test of the SR levels is met with weakness and an inability to break through, and then is followed by a strong price movement in the opposite direction.

The importance of head and shoulder formations is in the way that resistance (top pattern) and support (bottom pattern) are tested, and in the forecasting advantage that these patterns provide. Head and shoulders is one of the more popular methods for anticipating breakout of SR. The triple signal attempt at breakout, with each one failing, provides confirmation that, in fact, prices are going to head in the opposite direction.

Triangles

The triangle pattern, so called for its shape, is one continuation pattern closely associated with the establishment of a new SR and trading range; or, the triangle may precede a period of increased volatility.

Triangles may be symmetrical, descending or ascending. The symmetrical triangle, also called the coil, has a rising support line and a falling resistance line. The two lines converge near the middle of the initial range. The volume will often peak at the end of the trend just as or right before the triangle pattern starts to unfold. As the market moves sideways, the volume will continue to recede. If the volume is higher on the support side, this suggests that the market is likely to break through on the upside. On the other hand, if the heaviest volume appears when the prices are trading near resistance, and the price bars close near the lower end of the bar's range, a downside breakout can be anticipated. The symmetrical triangle typically indicates that, at least for the moment, buying and selling interests are balanced against one another.

Triangle: A pattern that may be symmetrical, ascending, or descending. The triangle is a continuation pattern which, when combined with an analysis of volume characteristics, can be used to anticipate near-term price movement.

Figure 4-5 shows Johnson & Johnson (JNJ) trading sideways as a symmetrical triangle. Volume declined during the triangle and then expanded as the price broke out.

The descending triangle has a falling resistance line and a horizontal support line. As the market moves sideways, the prices fail to achieve higher levels; yet, the support line holds. The volume characteristics are important to analyze along with the emerging triangle pattern, since the combination of price and volume are required to properly anticipate the

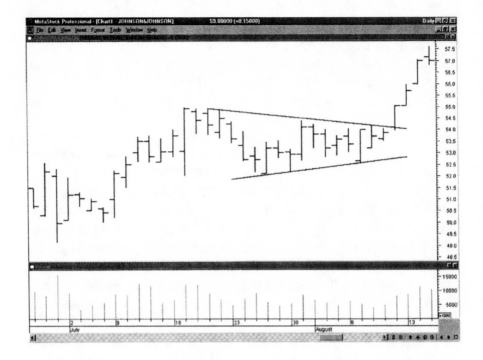

FIGURE 4-5

next price move direction. Despite the observation that support is holding throughout the development of the triangle, if the volume is heavier on the failed attempts to move through resistance, then support may collapse. In that instance, the inability of price to move through resistance even with heavy volume indicates that buyers are too scarce to create a breakout. The descending triangle is usually a bearish price pattern and, when confirmed with other information, can be used to anticipate a weakening price trend.

Figure 4-6 shows a descending triangle for Yahoo! (YHOO). The test of support saw a price rally with expanded volume. However, during the week of August 10, the price closed at the low for the

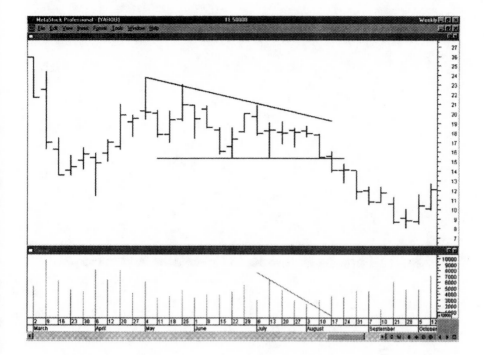

week and the volume broke the down-trend line, which anticipated a breakout below support.

FIGURE 4-6

The ascending triangle is composed of a rising support line and a horizontal resistance line. In this pattern, buyers are coming into the stock, creating higher and higher prices, while sellers hold at a fixed price level. Volume is essential to determining the significance to this price pattern. Heavy volume at resistance indicates weakening buyer activity and a possible downside breakout. If the volume is rising when price is at or near support, that may point to an impending breakout above resistance. The ascending triangle pattern is usually considered bullish and can be useful in anticipating an upward price trend.

If the volume is rising when price is at or near support, that may point to an impending breakout above resistance.

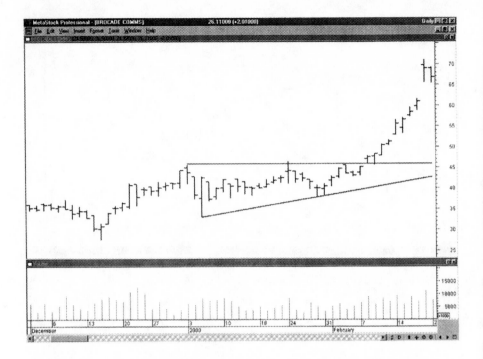

FIGURE 4-7

Figure 4-7, Brocade Communications (BRCD), traced out an ascending triangle before resuming another up leg in the trend.

One useful technique for trading a triangle is to plot the trend lines to the point they cross, and then determine the 50–66% range from the point where the triangle begins to the point where it ends. This 50–66% zone is the typical area that prices will exit the triangle. If the price stays within the confines of the triangle past this exit zone, the breakout will not develop into a longer-term trend.

Triangles are likely to serve only as short-term price indicators. They can anticipate SR breakouts, of course, and that is ultimately their usefulness. They should not be viewed for price patterns alone, however. An expected breakout should be confirmed by volume trends as explained above. If the corresponding volume changes are not found, then the triangle could be a short-term aberration or merely a coincidental and random pattern. When triangles are short-term in nature, they are more properly classified as flags.

Short Term and Intraday Patterns

Flags and short-term triangles are quick consolidation periods with tight boundaries of support and resistance that occur within existing trends. A flag is so named because the trading action has parallel support and resistance trend lines that are either horizontal or slope downward. Figure 4-8 is a

FIGURE 4-8

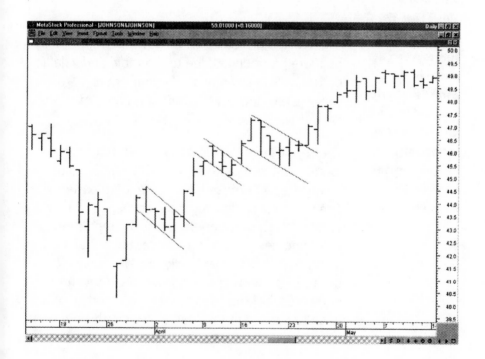

Flag: A short-term pattern usually caused by a pause in the trend, with a parallel shape sloping in a direction opposite the larger trend. The flag is useful for short-term analysis, but of questionable value as a long-term indicator.

Pennant: A short-term triangular pattern representing a pause in the established price trend. It is usually followed by a resumption of the price movement in the same direction.

30-minute bar chart of Johnson & Johnson showing a series of flags during the up trend.

The value of identifying flags often is in specifically distinguishing them as pausing in the established trend rather than as a sign of newly emerging trends. The short-term flag tends to slope in a direction opposite the trend. Thus, if prices are inching upward, the flag will have a downward shape, with a tendency for prices to climb upon completion of the flag's pattern.

A pennant looks like the triangle, but is usually shorter-term in duration, usually lasting no longer than a week or two. The pennant is a type of slowdown or pause in the price trend and usually is followed by a resumption of the previously established price movement direction.

Short term triangles, or pennants, often occur as brief pauses in a steep up or down trend, but may be more pronounced due to the rapid and volatile nature of that steep price change. Figure 4-9 shows CMGI Inc. (CMGI) with a number of short-term triangles during a larger down trend.

The classic chart patterns may occur not only in long-term trend patterns, but also in short-term daily price patterns or Intra-day trading patterns. The technical analyst faces the challenge of trying to distinguish between patterns that represent emerging new trends, and those that are only false starts. This is the great challenge, of course, because as trends emerge, it is more difficult to interpret them than it is to look back and identify what happened in the past. However, this does not

FIGURE 4-9

mean that seemingly brief or short-term patterns can be ignored; they may be the beginning of important reversals. Many price swings on stocks begin from Intra-day chart patterns. Figure 4-10 is the 30-minute chart of AT&T, showing a double top formed before the price fell from $20 to below $18. Figure 4-11 shows trading the 30-minute chart for Microsoft (MSFT), which formed a symmetrical triangle as a reversal pattern.

Gaps

A gap is a space in between price range from one day to the next. For example, if a stock trades today between $18 and $21 per share, but opens tomorrow at $23, a two-point gap occurred.

The technical analyst faces the challenge of trying to distinguish between patterns that represent emerging new trends, and those that are only false starts.

FIGURE 4-10

Gaps can be interpreted in three different ways. A breakaway gap signals a strong market move. For example, if the gap occurs above the neckline of a head and shoulders bottom, that could strongly confirm the head and shoulders trend.

Gap: A space between daily trading ranges from one day to the next, significant because it may signal important changes in price trading patterns.

A second interpretation is called the runaway gap, which occurs within an established trend, normally one in which prices are rising or falling strongly. The third type of gap, an exhaustion gap, is likely to occur at the end of a strong price trend and could indicate that the trend is about to end out. For example, if prices have been climbing rapidly and strongly, an exhaustion gap may signal that prices are about to top. This type of gap may be

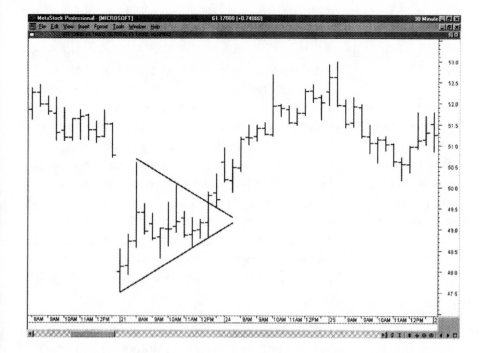

followed shortly by a breakaway gap heading in
the opposite direction. Together, this pattern, often
called an island reversal, is a sign that prices are
going to head in the opposite direction.

FIGURE 4-11

Summary

Chart patterns may serve as indicators that continue or reverse established SR and trading ranges.
It is not a simple matter to distinguish short-term
or false starts from the stronger and more permanent changes in price direction. The key is to study
volume trends along with those price patterns. The
two together are more likely to anticipate breakout
or confirm the current SR range.

In order to more thoroughly understand the nature of SR and *why* price may breakout and establish a new trading range, the study of interim patterns is a useful exercise. As prices test SR levels, volume trends confirm what the price pattern appears to imply; however, every technician also needs to remember that there is a random element to short-term price movement. Not every pattern is significant. It is prudent to always watch volume as well, and to ensure that the elements of price movement—SR tests, price spikes at top or bottom, head and shoulders patterns, and triangles—are interpreted properly, and are not misunderstood in error. The value in price movement patterns is always confirmed when SR is tested and either holds or is broken.

Every technician also needs to remember that there is a random element to short-term price movement.

With that observation in mind, how can you best use price patterns to take advantage of extremely short-term changes? The next chapter shows how swing trading puts these valuable patterns to work.

CHAPTER 5

Swing Trading: Creating Maximum Profit Opportunities

Y ou can use chart patterns to time your entry and exit points. By analyzing consecutive high and low points and spotting SR test signals, you can invest as prices swing from one direction to the other. As a "swing trader," you combine well-known price patterns with gaps, volume analysis and confirmation signals, to anticipate which direction prices are going to take.

One popular swing trading method is based on a three-bar pattern demonstrating peaks with three higher highs, or dips with three lower lows.[1] For example, Figure 5-1 shows an upswing as the price bars achieve higher highs, but when the bars make three lower lows, the swing turns down. Once the swing turns direction, the highs or lows do not have to be consecutive. If the market traces out two higher highs and the next high is a lower high, and then prices rally to another new high, the swing is still up. A swing chart determines the trend by tracking the highs and lows. Whether consecutive or not, the pattern is established by

Swing trade: A trade timed to anticipate a swing in price movement from one direction to the other, so that entry and exit are timed based on pattern signals.

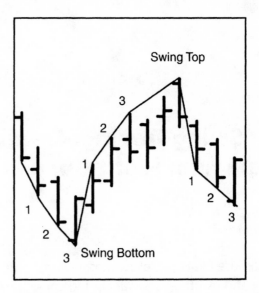

FIGURE 5-1

highs outpacing previous levels, or lows declining below previous levels.

Support and Resistance

On Figure 5-1, the support point is the swing bottom as prices moved from a downswing to an upswing. If movement were taking place in the opposite direction, the resistance point would be identified as the point where an upspring reversed into a downswing. As with all cases of patterns, SR levels are established by unsuccessful attempts to break through, and these are usually followed by a reversal in price movement.

3-bar Swings versus 2-bar Swings

Some traders have observed significant differences between swings lasting over two bars and those

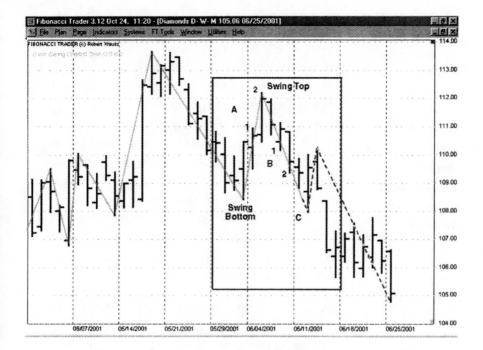

FIGURE 5-2

taking three bars. According to these traders, two bar swings are preferable to three-bar swings because the likelihood of picking and timing the impending movement correctly is stronger with the shorter-term swing pattern.[2] Figure 5-2 shows a two-bar swing chart.

According to proponents of the preferred two-bar method, if and when a two-bar swing top is violated, the trend turns up. If a two-bar swing bottom is broken, then the trend turns down. Figure 5-2 shows an example within the box on the chart. At point A, two consecutive higher highs precede an upturn of the swing. At point B, two consecutive lower lows precede a downturn of the swing line, and a swing top is established. At point C, the

The long position exit should be made when resistance appears to weaken, and short positions should be closed when support appears about to erode and give way.

previous swing bottom is violated so the trend turns down and the swing line is dashed.

Reviews of charts show well-defined up trends as a series of rising support swing bottoms (support points). Downtrends consist of falling swing tops (resistance points). By applying the definition of the trend to the chart, the swing trader can time entry into long positions at the bottom of the channel, or right at support, or short positions at the top where resistance is established. On the closing side, the long position exit should be made when resistance appears to weaken, and short positions should be closed when support appears about to erode and give way.

Swing traders may advance this technique by using multiple time frames alone or in combination. For example, your current trading pattern could be set using daily bars, and the next time frame would be the weekly bars. By using a multiple time approach, you are able to differentiate between major and minor signals. Swing tops and bottoms would be interpreted as major SR on a weekly basis and minor support and resistance on a daily basis, for example.

Figure 5-3 (Microsoft) shows that the Weekly Gann Swing is up, but the trend is down (dashed lines) indicating that prices recently broke a weekly swing bottom. The Daily Swing Lines are solid and form a swing bottom. When prices broke the swing bottom, the Daily Swing Trend came into agreement with the indicators on the Weekly Swing Trend. With this information, breakouts of major SR levels would be more easily identified than minor SR probes, providing you with useful confirming signals.

Gann Swing Chartist Next NQM

Daily Gann Swing is Up
and the Trend is up.

Swing Bottom is
broken and daily
trend turns down.

Swing bottom
(support)

Weekly Gann Swing is Up
but the Trend is down.

FIBONACCI TRADER (c) Robert Krausz

Other Swing Trading Concepts

FIGURE 5-3

Many swing traders have further observed that up trending markets tend to move in patterns exhibiting swings of higher highs and higher lows.[3] By using specific setups for entering into trades based on market direction, swing traders can employ the strategy of simply watching for consecutive lower highs or consecutive higher lows.

Once the price reaches a new high it may be followed by three to five consecutive lower highs. This downswing is due to late buyers coming in and buying at the short-term top. As the market moves lower, the same late buyers will be likely to exit their positions to cut their losses. The same strategy works on the downside. Once the price falls to a new low it may be followed by three to five consecutive higher lows. Similarly, following market action presents the short seller with timing opportunities.

This type of trading action is typical of the majority of market followers, who chronically buy after a price peak and sell only to cut losses. This presents the astute swing trader with an opportunity to take positions in the up trend by buying after this series of three to five consecutive lower highs or higher lows. This variation on swing trading is a chartist's version of contrarian investing—going against the action of the market. By timing long or short entry to consecutive lower highs or consecutive higher lows, the contrarian swing trader is able to take advantage of the common trading patterns of market reaction.

For example, Figure 5-4 is Affymetrix. This market had been making higher highs and higher lows. The expectation is that this pattern represents a new support point in a general up trend. If the support point does not hold, the swing trader should exit with a small loss. Partial profits can be taken when the market returns to the old high, and a trailing stop order placed for the remainder of the position.

For stocks in a down trend consisting of a series of lower lows and lower highs, look for stocks that have rallied with three to five consecutive higher lows.

For stocks in a down trend consisting of a series of lower lows and lower highs, look for stocks that have rallied with three to five consecutive higher lows. Here, a stock may be advancing because buyers believe that the market has come down too far too fast and may be making a bottom—this is believed despite the fact the market is clearly in a down trend. For example, Figure 5-5 shows Yahoo

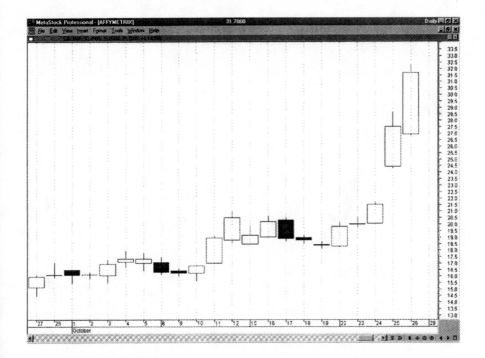

(YHOO) in a downtrend with a short term rally consisting of four higher highs, after which the price rolled over again.

FIGURE 5-4

Traders who buy against the trend will likely sell out quickly if the trade does not work. This presents another opportunity. If the price trades below the low third or higher consecutive low, the contrarian swing trader may go short and remain at risk up to the high of the entry bar or the previous bar, whichever is higher. In this trade, the setup takes advantage of a potential resistance level just as it is forming. If the resistance level does form, then prices should fall to new lows typical of the down trend. Partial profits can then be taken near

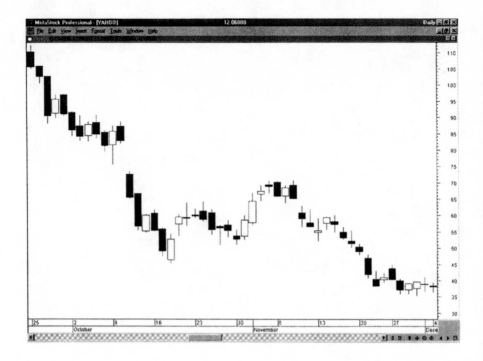

FIGURE 5-5   the previous low, entering a trailing stop for the remainder of the position.

Summary

Swing trading takes maximum advantage of the tendency for prices to ebb and flow in the short term, to move in directions against the trend, and to reestablish that trend again. By waiting for the counter trends to occur and then trading in the direction of the trend, you create many more short-term profit opportunities. Swing trading utilizes SR as points to enter stop losses for trades, as well as targets for profit-taking.

This is the essence of swing trading, and ultimately it defines your success in technical market trading. Beyond the short-term effectiveness of swing trading techniques, you can employ the same skills to forecast likely SR trends into the immediate future. The next chapter shows how to spot the signals for emerging SR trends.

NOTES

1 This system was developed in the 1930s by trader W. D. Gann

2 Krausz, Robert, *A W. D. Gann Treasure Discovered,* citing a handwritten W. D. Gann trading course

3 Velez, Oliver, and Greg Capra, *Tools and Tactics for the Master Day Trader*

CHAPTER 6

Learning to Forecast SR Levels

C an we forecast SR levels? Many technical methods offer an objective or target on the completion of a particular pattern or technique. You can think of these targets as forecasted SR levels. In this section, we review chart pattern targets, ratio analysis, and the Elliott Wave technique.

Target: A price range expected in the near future based on current trading signals within chart patterns.

Chart Pattern Measured Movements

In the head and shoulders pattern (Figure 6-1), prediction is possible because the pattern itself is such a strong indicator. By measuring the difference between the neckline and the head (A-B) and anticipating that the price will move through the neckline, we can anticipate that the price will fall at least as far below the neckline (B-C) as the difference between the top of the head to the neckline. This symmetrical offsetting pattern is a popular technique used by many chartists. The expectation in a head and shoulders bottom is the same. If the neckline is violated, the market should rise an equal distance above the neckline as the difference

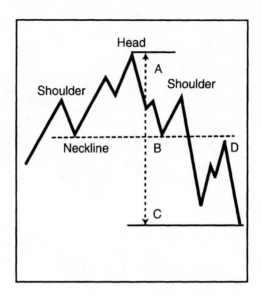

FIGURE 6-1

between the head and the neckline. This price area then becomes a target. In addition, when the neckline is first penetrated, prices may retest the neckline (Point D) before continuing the new trend. Typically, the volume during the retracement is low, implying a counter trend movement.

For the double or triple top, the difference between the extreme price of the pattern and the support points occurring between the price peaks is the starting point for anticipating a price target.

The double and triple top or bottom patterns are subject to the same price patterns. For the double (Figure 6-2) or triple top, the difference between the extreme price of the pattern and the support points occurring between the price peaks (A-B) is the starting point for anticipating a price target. When the support point gives way, this difference is subtracted from the support level (B-C), and that becomes the target within this pattern. Increased volume with a weakening support level indicates that sellers are picking up momentum.

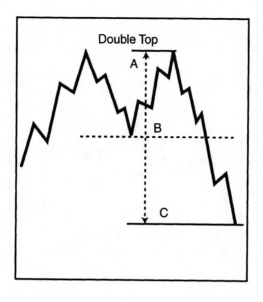

FIGURE 6-2

The double or triple bottom objective is the difference between the extreme low and the resistance level formed between the low points. If the market trades through the resistance level then the difference is added to the resistance level, to identify the new target or next resistance level.

Larger triangles, which form over several weeks or even months, have a measured target. Targets can be set for symmetrical, ascending, and descending triangles with the same technique. The widest vertical range in the triangle is added to the apex for an upside breakout or subtracted from the apex for a downside breakout. For example, in Figure 6-3, subtract the difference between points A and B and then add this difference to the apex (C to D).

For short-term triangle and flag formations, the same techniques are used to identify an initial

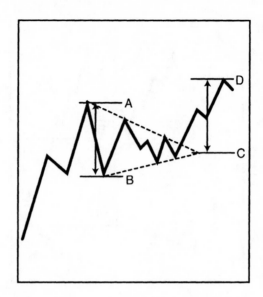

FIGURE 6-3

target. However, as shown in Figures 4-8 and 4-9 (see Chapter 4), short term flags and triangles may develop quickly, so using a trailing stop rather than a target price could be more profitable.

Traders may identify targets based on chart patterns, especially reversal patterns, as a first objective in the trend. Therefore, many traders take partial profits when the target is hit, and then move their stop loss point to the initial entry price. If the market reverses, profits are locked in on a part of the position and are at breakeven on the remainder. If the market continues the trend, a trailing stop can be used to exit the remainder of the position.

Ratio Analysis

Technicians use ratios to calculate future SR levels. The most common approach looks for a 50%

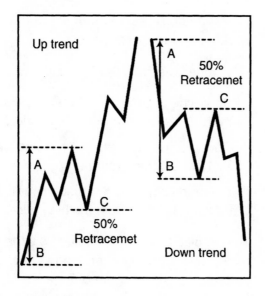

FIGURE 6-4

retracement of the previous swing. For example, Figure 6-4 shows two cases, one for an up trend and one for a downtrend. The counter trend movement is expected to retrace 50% of the previous swing from points A to B, and then to C.

A method identified by one trader is called the "Rule of Seven," a formula used to set price objectives.[1] First, calculate the difference between the high and the low of the initial upswing, multiply the difference by seven, divide the product by four, and add that to the low for the first objective. For the second objective repeat the steps but divide by three, and for the third objective divide by two. Here are the formulas:

Upside objective #1: High minus low, multiply by 1.75, add to low price.

Upside objective #2: High minus low, multiply by 2.33, add to low price.

Upside objective #3: High minus low, multiply by 3.50, add to low price.

Downside objectives use 5, 4 and 3 for the divisor:

Downside objective #1: High minus low, multiply by 1.40, subtract from the high price.

Downside objective #2: High minus low, multiply by 1.75, subtract from the high price.

Downside objective #3: High minus low, multiply by 2.33, subtract from the high price.

These objectives can be applied to either swing measurements or for confirmation of classic chart pattern objectives. Figure 6-5 is a weekly chart of Boeing. Points A to B is the first leg up from the

FIGURE 6-5

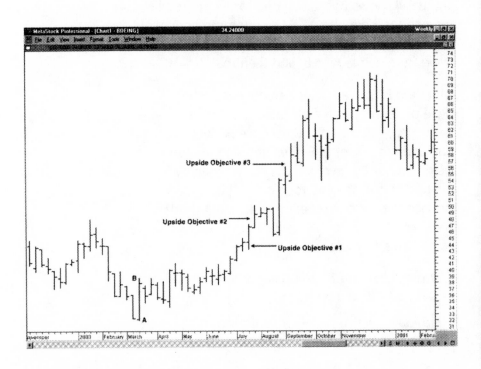

SUPPORT AND RESISTANCE SIMPLIFIED

bottom where the high has a lower high preceding and following it, and the low has a higher low preceding and following it. The difference in price is $38.9375 − $32 = $6.9375. Therefore, by applying the Rule of Seven to project the targets, objective 1 is $32 + (1.75 × $6.9375) = $44.14; upside objective 2 is $32 + (2.33 × $6.9375) = $48.16, upside objective 3 is $32 + (3.50 × $6.9375) = $56.28.

Figure 6-6 is an example of the Rule of Seven for downside objectives from a top using a weekly chart of Boeing. Swing A to B is $70.9375 − $54.56 = $16.38. Objective 1 is $70.9375 − (1.40 × $16.38) = $48.00 Objective 2 is $70.9375 − (1.75 × $16.38) = $42.28; Objective 3 is $70.9375 − (2.33 × $16.38) = $32.78.

FIGURE 6-6

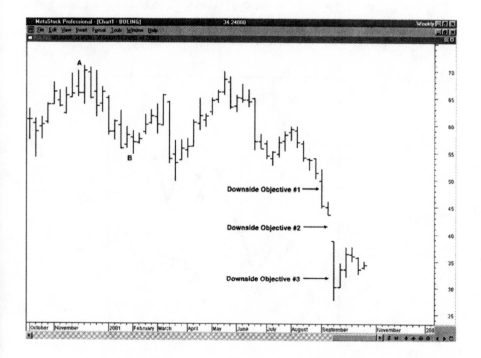

Fibonacci Targets

Technicians also employ ratios derived from a mathematical phenomenon called the Fibonacci series. This series is a sum of the previous two numbers (0, 1, 1, 2, 3, 5, 8, 13, 21 . . .). If you calculate the ratios of two numbers in a series you will note the progression is 100%, 50%, 66%, 62.5%, 61.5% . . . 61.8%. Calculating the difference between 100% and 61.8% is 38.2%. The Fibonacci series is considered the basis for naturally occurring change. Technicians have developed many elaborate uses of the ratios. One of the most complex is the Elliott Wave.

Elliott Wave

The Elliott Wave up trend consists of five waves or swings (Figure 6-7). Waves 1, 3 and 5 are considered impulse (trend) and waves 2 and 4 are corrective

FIGURE 6-7

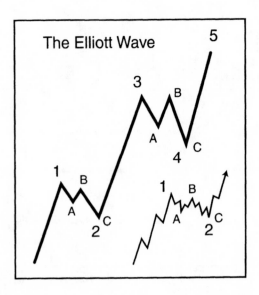

The Elliott Wave

(counter trend) waves. Wave 1 peaks, with resistance at the top of wave 1, and wave 2 corrects
wave 1. Wave 2 can be expected to retrace any-
where from 38.2 to 61.8% of wave 1, and sometimes back to the origin point. If wave 2 retraces all
of wave 1, a double bottom is formed.

As the peak of wave 1 is surpassed, resistance may
give way, and the price would then accelerate. This
is typical after resistance level breakout. Wave 3 is
often the longest of the waves. Followers of the
Elliott Wave often project that wave 3 will complete a new higher level for resistance, which
would then form a Fibonacci expansion of wave 1,
such as 138.2% to 261.8% of wave 1 (Figure 6-8).

The peak of wave 3 establishes a new level of
resistance, and wave 4 corrects wave 3. Wave 4
establishes a new support level. Wave 4 is
expected to unfold in some manner different from

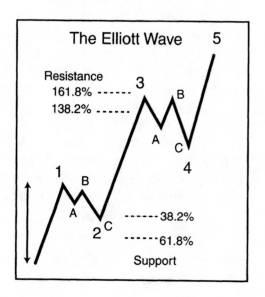

FIGURE 6-8

the characteristic of wave 2. For example, if wave 2 was deep, retracing 61.8% of wave 1, then wave 4 may be shallow and only retrace 38.2% of wave 3.

Wave 4 should be expected to retrace back to the support level formed when wave 3 completed its internal wave 4 level. Wave 4 is complete and wave 5 breaks through the resistance level (wave 3's peak). The peak of wave 5 will form a new resistance level. Elliott Wave technicians will project wave 5 peak to be a ratio related to the height of wave 3, or from the height of the beginning of wave 1 to the peak of wave 3.

SR levels are significant factors in computations and projections under the Elliott Wave technique, invariably based upon the relationships explained under the Fibonacci ratio relationships.

Summary

Patterns emerge in prices that can be useful for making informed target projections. Assuming that price patterns are themselves dependable, the methods developed by technicians can be used as first signs of an emerging target, or as confirmation for more familiar patterns, such as head and shoulders patterns or strong testing of SR levels.

As much intelligence as you gather from this study of price, it is only one aspect of the larger question. You improve your analytical skills with the combined study of price and volume trends. This idea is the topic of the next chapter.

NOTE

1 Sklarew, *Techniques of a Professional Chartist*

CHAPTER 7

Volume: The Other Confirmation Measure

onfirmation remains the key to SR analysis and to all other forms of price study, notably when trying to anticipate target levels. Confirmation is especially important when trading decisions are going to be made based on what appears to be going on with price.

However, price alone does not reveal every form of confirmation. Volume and the way that it changes is also critical in validating a breakout from SR levels. For example, if the neckline of a head and shoulders top is broken, the technician would expect to see an increase in volume as prices rise. This volume trend associated with price breakout serves as a confirming indicator in establishing the change in a trend.

Volume analysis can also serve as an indicator that disproves what appears to be happening in the price movement. For example, if the volume does not increase during a breakout from SR, then what otherwise appears as solid evidence may be considered suspect and due to some event unrelated to the stock or simply a false indicator. For example, a

Climax: A peak in trading volume signaling the end of the current trend and anticipating a price movement reversal.

broad market index such as the Dow Jones Industrial Average may break through resistance and many stocks may breakout as well. However, some may bid up due to crowd mentality, while others may move higher due to improving fundamentals and institutional buying activity. While breakouts accompanied by a substantial increase in volume are solid confirming signals, an apparent breakout with low volume may be a false indicator, and a retreat back to the established trading range is likely.

Volume should change in a consistent and measurable form if it is to be considered as confirming information.

Volume should change in a consistent and measurable form if it is to be considered as confirming information. For up trends, the volume will expand in the direction of the trend, and during pull backs or consolidations, the volume numbers will recede. However, if the volume reaches an unusually high level in a short period of time, that could signal the culmination of the trend and serve as a contrary signal. This buying or selling climax would predict a reversal.

A bottom may take the shape of a two-step process forming a major support level and involving changes in volume. A bottom formation took place in Diamonds (DIA), in March of 2001 shown in Figure 7-1. The first leg was a climatic sell-off. Here, institutional investors liquidated their long positions at Point A. Next, the market rallied as short position holders took profits. The rally stalled, and the price retreated back down to the low, retesting the first bottom. During this decline, the volume did not expand, indicating that there were no more sellers in response to the lower prices (Point B). Technicians call this a sold out market. The major support level was established at the heavy volume day. At this

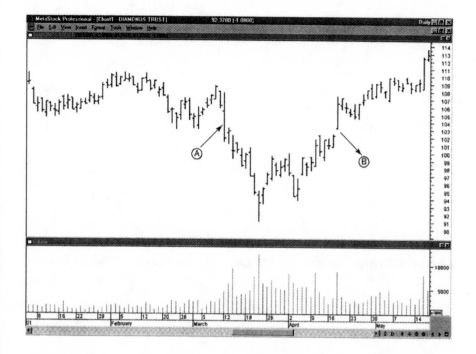

FIGURE 7-1

point, the market has discounted all of the negative
fundamentals and formed a major support level. A
market top started with a buying climax (Figure 7-2,
Point A). Here, the news had been positive, and
more and more buyers jumped onto the trend.
Profit-taking caused a decline in price, retracing
38% to 50% of the previous rally. After this, the
price began to advance, retesting the first major
resistance level, but this time volume did not rise as
higher prices were paid (Point B). This anemic retest
of the previous high indicated that everyone who
could have bought was already long. Resistance was
set one day after the big volume day, and a second,
lower resistance level followed. Any negative news
at that point would have caused profit-taking. If the
news had been negative, the likelihood of a major

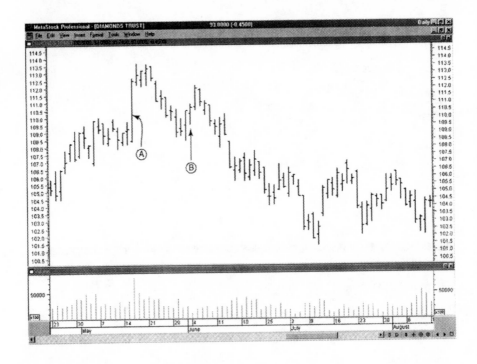

FIGURE 7-2

top was high. Major resistance had been established on the charts.

Volume Indicators

Technicians have developed a host of volume-based indicators to confirm a breakout of SR levels. The most common is the on-balance volume indicator (OBV) developed by Joe Granville.[1] This is the running sum of the cumulative volume weighted by whether the market closes up or down for the day. If the market closes up, then the entire day's volume is added to the previous day's OBV value. If the market closes down, then the entire day's volume is subtracted from the previous day's OBV value. Traders look for the OBV line to confirm breakouts and the trend. Thus, if the market breaks

SUPPORT AND RESISTANCE SIMPLIFIED

out of a trading range, then the OBV line should break out as well. As an even stronger indicator, the OBV may lead and, thus, anticipate the price breakout. Once in an up trend, the OBV line should steadily rise as the price trends higher. If the OBV line begins to diverge, tracing out lower highs while the market is making new highs, a reversal of the trend is anticipated.

For market tops, when prices break, a key support line the OBV line should also break. It is even a stronger indicator if the OBV trend precedes the price. A down-trending OBV line indicates that more volume is occurring on down closing days than on up closing days. If price continues to trade

FIGURE 7-3

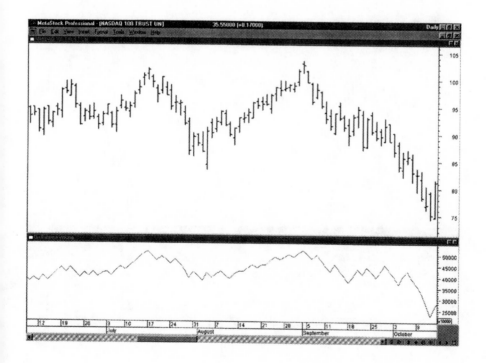

within its trading range, the OBV line may predict the direction that price can be expected to move in the coming breakout. Figure 7-3 is the Nasdaq 100 Trust (QQQ). The daily chart edged to a new high in September, but the OBV Line stopped at the previous high. Next, as the QQQ began to work lower, the OBV line broke through support before the same move in price, a good example of the OBV leading. One problem with the OBV indicator is the price may close down just a few cents for the day, causing all of that day's volume to be subtracted from the OBV line. The calculation is an all-or-nothing without weight being given for volume variations. The accumulation/distribution line[2] is another indicator that weights the volume by the percentage placement of the closing price relative

FIGURE 7-4

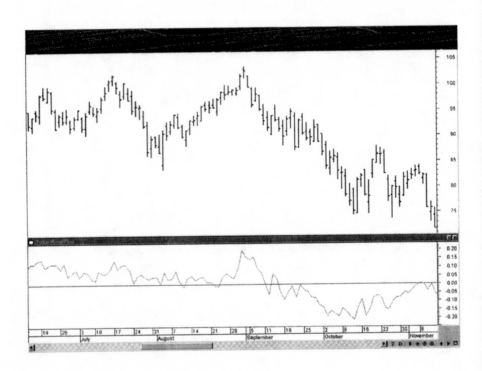

to the day's range, and then adds that adjusted volume number to the previous day's accumulation/ distribution line. This indicator takes into account where the market is closing each day and tracks volume accordingly. Most technicians view the accumulation/distribution line as superior to the OBV line based on the weighted volume. The accumulation/distribution line was improved further by taking the sum of the weighted volume over the applicable period and dividing it by total volume. Figure 7-4 illustrates a positive reading that confirms a breakout above resistance.

Summary

The level of volume accompanying breakout below support or above resistance provides confirmation of the breakout; or a lack of corresponding volume increases serves as an indicator that those breakouts are false and will retrace. The addition of volume-based indicators vastly improves the technician's ability to accurately predict price movement.

Remember, though, that the forward-looking analysis of price and volume serve only to improve your outcome, not to completely eliminate risk. We have to accept the reality that the whole purpose of this study is to improve our predicting and analytical skills. The next chapter summarizes modern trends in the science of SR.

NOTE

1 Granville, Joe, *New Strategy of Daily Stock Market Timing for Maximum Profits*

2 Developed by Larry Williams and later improved upon by Marc Chaikin

CHAPTER 8

Applying Modern Innovations to SR Applications

The science of technical analysis is constantly in a state of change and development. The widespread availability of online information and home computers, for example, has made even complex mathematical computations automatic, easy, and accessible. Real-time chart pattern analysis, moving average computation, and turnover analysis are all simple in comparison to the manual systems used in the past.

One modern innovation is a form of turnover analysis, which compares outstanding shares of stock to trends in the trading range. This is called the Woods Cumulative-Volume Float Indicator. It compares a running sum of the volume relative to the available float of shares outstanding, to the trading ranges established or changed each time the entire float turns over (on average).[1]

The "turnover" is an average. The calculation does not require a complete change of ownership but does represent the trading of a number of shares equal to total outstanding shares. For example, a stock has a float of 10 million shares. From July 1 to

August 1 the trading volume was 10.1 million shares, and the range of prices was a high of $21 to $14. In this example, the entire float of stock has turned over; in fact, actual turnover is 1.01 times (10.1 divided by 10). According to this technical theory, it is considered to be very significant if price breaks the support or resistance level established during the period required for one complete turnover of the float. For example, if the stock price has been in a down trend and then drops to a price low enough that institutional buyers consider it a bargain, they will accumulate positions in the stock. That creates more rapid turnover which, in effect, was caused by the breakout below support.

Prices will tend to advance following institutional buy decisions, as individual or retail investors follow suit. Under the theory, the shares have changed hands as part of a support breakout, and subsequent bargain buying forms a new bottom level for that stock.

If the market has been in an up trend and the entire float turns over, then a new market top is created as resistance is broken and a new level created above.

When the market is trending up, the resistance levels are broken and higher support levels are established. Float Channel Lines connecting the right hand corner of the SR levels identify each turnover period. The Float Channel Lines mark the SR boundaries. Figure 8-1 illustrates an example of the Float Channel Lines for market bottoms, tops and trends. When the market is trending up, these Float Channel Lines trend up as well, but if the

Understanding Float Analysis

The Float [aka the floating supply of shares] - the number of freely traded shares in the hands of the public; shares outstanding less shares owned by the management.

Float Turnover - a "proxy" for a change in ownership. The amount of time it takes for a stock's cumulative volume to equal its floating supply of shares and the price range of same. It implies that a large percentage of the stock's ownership has changed hands. A new technical term created by Steve Woods to help explain his discoveries.

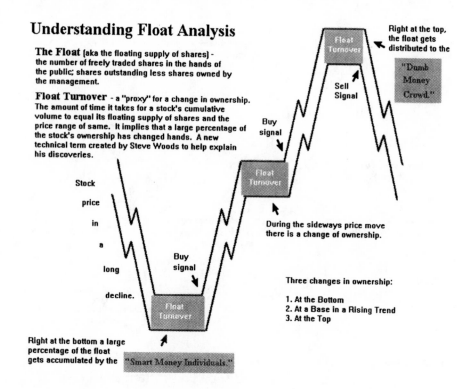

market trades sideways and the support level determined by the turnover of the float gives way, then a market top is confirmed.

FIGURE 8-1

Down trending markets are followed by the stair stepping downward Float Channel Lines. As the market moves sideways, the Float Channel Lines establish the significant SR levels. A major bottom is established when the float turnover resistance level is broken. Figure 8-2, Juniper Networks (JNPR), shows an example of such a market bottom. During the month of September and early October, 2001, there was a complete turnover of the share float. The two horizontal lines represent the high and low of the price range during that period. In early

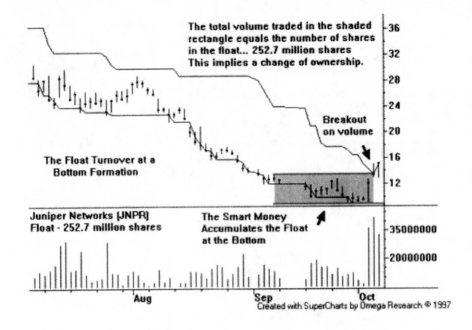

The total volume traded in the shaded rectangle equals the number of shares in the float... 252.7 million shares This implies a change of ownership.

Breakout on volume

The Float Turnover at a Bottom Formation

Juniper Networks (JNPR) Float - 252.7 million shares

The Smart Money Accumulates the Float at the Bottom

Aug

FIGURE 8-2

October, Juniper closed above the Float Channel Line. Figure 8-3 shows a substantial gain during the days immediately following the breakout.

Intermarket Analysis

A rising interest rate environment may have a negative influence on the stock market because higher interest rates raise expense for business and cut into profits. In addition, investors may begin to view debt securities as more attractive than equities, so capital tends to move out of stocks and into bonds. If interest rates fall, the opposite may occur, with more capital moving into stocks and creating greater buying pressure. Given these general observations, it is fair to note that the stock market often is a lagging indicator of the interest rate market. Technicians have observed this linkage

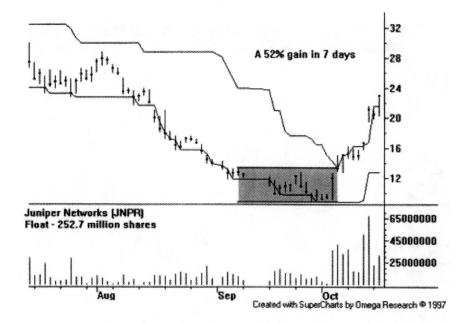

A 52% gain in 7 days

Juniper Networks (JNPR)
Float - 252.7 million shares

Aug   Sep   Oct

Created with SuperCharts by Omega Research © 1997

among markets, and those observations have become the basis for several technical theories concerning SR analysis.[2]

FIGURE 8-3

Technicians applying intermarket analysis use a combination of trend analysis and major breaks of key SR points to identify changes in the trend and to illustrate how these changes may impact other markets. Using market interest rates as an example, compare the two-year T-note Futures contract (Figure 8-4) and the NASDAQ 100 Index (Figure 8-5). When the price of a two-year T-note is falling the yield is climbing. In late 1998, the price of the two-year T-note was rising (interest rates were falling) and the NASDAQ market ended a decline and advanced until the first quarter of 2000. The T-note broke support (point A) and falling prices (rising rates) indicated that the economy was strong, at which point the NASDAQ

Technicians applying inter-market analysis use a combination of trend analysis and major breaks of key SR points to identify changes in the trend.

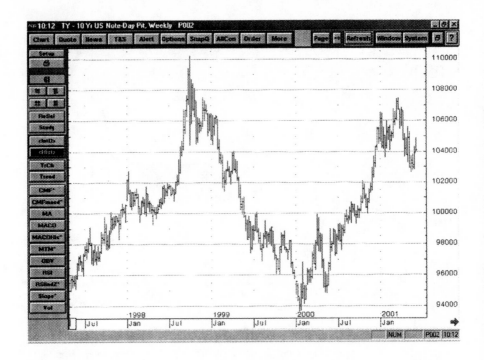

FIGURE 8-4

100 index continued to advance. The T-note reached a bottom in January 2000 and then broke through resistance (point B). The NASDAQ 100 Index topped in March of 2000, and formed a lower high (point C, Figure 8-5). The fact that the trend of the T-note was down was a clear indication that the stock market was due for a serious retracement. However, the NASDAQ 100 Index plummeted, and the two-year T-note price rose, demonstrating how one market may affect another.

T-note prices rose as the economy continued to expand, which was one reason why the NASDAQ 100 Index continued to climb. However, as interest rates continued moving, the economy slowed, and the NASDAQ 100 Index fell on falling earnings

expectations. As the NASDAQ 100 Index fell, interest rates began to fall as well, and falling stock
market levels induced investors to buy T-notes
rather than leaving capital in stocks. By observing
the interaction between key SR levels, you can
identify the important inter-market trends as they
begin to emerge.

FIGURE 8-5

Sector and Group Analysis

A "top down" technical approach based on Index
rather than stock analysis is another popular modern technique, especially for market-wide technical
analysis. This starts with identification of the leading market sector, group or industry and then
determining the leaders from within those groups.

Watching for the breaks of key SR levels may point to the more profitable stocks to trade. A leading group or sector may show that a number of stocks trend in the same direction at the same time, but the real leaders will exhibit the best relative strength compared to the group index and to the market as a whole. Watching how SR levels give way or hold offers clear insight into the technical health of the stock.

For example, during the summer of 2001 the S&P 500 trended lower, breaking the March support level, while the biotech index held above March support (Figure 8-6). The better relative strength of the biotech index was an important indication

FIGURE 8-6

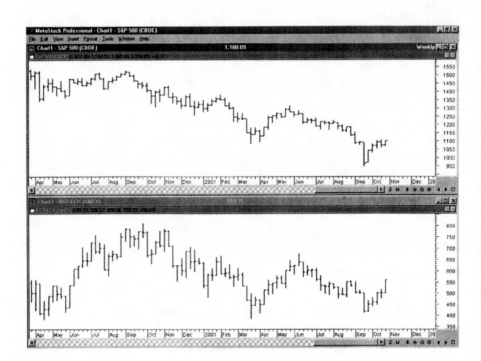

SUPPORT AND RESISTANCE SIMPLIFIED

that the biotech sector had higher relative strength than the broader S&P 500.

Summary

Many aspects of technical analysis are built upon the concepts of SR trends, from chart patterns to trend lines. These trends provide dependable confirming or contradicting signals that every technician can employ to strengthen a belief about impending price movement. The use of modern techniques, as well as traditional tried and true chart patterns, enables the technician to grasp the rhythm of price movement, especially as it relates to SR trends. We may view the trading range, defined by support on the bottom and resistance on the top, as the sensible trading range reflected in the interaction between buyers and sellers, which should remain dependably stable until one side or the other gives way. For very low-volatility stocks, such short-term trends are unlikely because there is little market interest in moving price in either direction. For highly volatile stocks, no form of analysis will work, because the instability and chaos in present price movement cannot be predicted.

Just as any form of technical analysis is easily evaluated in hindsight, we must strive to remember that the real challenge is in the interpretation of emerging, new information. Looking ahead and attempting to anticipate the degree and direction of the next price change is where technicians make or break their theory. The successful technical analyst is not going to be correct all of the time. However, being right more often than being wrong is enough of an edge for most people—it puts you ahead of the averages.

NOTES

1 Woods, Steve, the Woods Cumulative-Volume Float Indicator, *The Precision Profit Float Indicator*

2 Murphy, John, *Intermarket Analysis* and Martin Pring, *The All-Season Investor: Successful Strategies for Every Stage in the Business Cycle*

Glossary

accumulation area

A price range in which buying activity is taking place, indicating growing support.

breakout

A price movement above resistance or below support, often the signal that a new trading range is being formed in the stock pricing pattern.

climax

A peak in trading volume signaling the end of the current trend and anticipating a price movement reversal.

confirmation

A signal or indicator that supports a previous signal and thus adds to the evidence that a specific technical change is occurring in a price trend.

consolidation

A temporarily slowing of price movement and narrowing of trading range, awaiting realignment of buyers and sellers.

continuation pattern

A pattern that reinforces the current price trend, including pauses in price movement followed by a resumption of the previous direction.

distribution area

A price range in which trading is taking place over a longer than average time, in which sellers want to support prices to avoid a decline.

double bottom

A chart pattern characterized by two price drops testing support, with a price rise in between. The unsuccessful test of support is viewed as a bullish sign, often anticipating a breakout above previous resistance levels.

double top

A chart pattern characterized by two price peaks testing resistance, with a decline in between. The unsuccessful test of resistance is viewed as a bearish sign, often anticipating a breakout below previous support levels.

flag

A short-term pattern usually caused by a pause in the trend, with a parallel shape sloping in a direction opposite the larger trend. The flag is useful for short-term analysis but of questionable value as a long-term indicator.

gap

A space between daily trading ranges from one day to the next, significant because it may signal important changes in price trading patterns.

head and shoulders pattern

A chart pattern resembling a left and right plateau with a higher center plateau (head and shoulders top) or the reverse (head and shoulders bottom), with a middle lower trading level and higher plateaus trading before and after.

neckline

The trading area in a head and shoulders pattern found between the head and each of the two shoulders.

pennant

A short-term triangular pattern representing a pause in the established price trend. It is usually followed by a resumption of the price movement in the same direction.

pivot high or low

The price point at which support or resistance are tested unsuccessfully, after which prices retrace back toward the middle of the trading range.

primary trend

The main movement in the market, usually lasting for months or even years, establishing an overall direction for broadly-based price trends.

resistance

The highest price or price trend at which a stock is trading currently in its trading range; the price that buyers consider the highest worthwhile price for that stock.

resistance point

A point in a price pattern in which resistance is tested unsuccessfully by prices attempting to break higher.

retracement

A movement in prices in the opposite direction from a recent trend.

reversal pattern

A pattern preceding a change in direction of price movement, or the breaking of a previously established trading range.

support

The lowest price or price trend at which a stock is trading currently in its trading range; the price that buyers currently consider the lowest worthwhile price for that stock.

support point

A point in a price pattern in which support is tested successfully by prices attempting to break lower.

swing trade

A trade timed to anticipate a swing in price movement from one direction to the other, so that entry and exit are timed based on pattern signals.

target

A price range expected in the near future based on current trading signals within chart patterns.

trading range

The level of trading in a stock, topped by the price resistance level and bottomed by the price support level.

triangle

A pattern that may be symmetrical, ascending, or descending. The triangle is a continuation pattern which, when combined with an analysis of volume characteristics, can be used to anticipate near-term price movement.

Educational Resources

RECOMMENDED READING

Advanced Swing Trading

by John Crane

In *Advanced Swing Trading,* John Crane, a veteran trader and co-founder of "Traders Network," discusses his work with Action/Reaction trading theory and illustrates a whole new way of using time, price, and patterns to predict, identify, and trade future market swings.

$69.95   *Item #T186X-1199048*

Swing Trading: Power Strategies to Cut Risk and Boost Profits

by Jon Markman

Ideal for today's active traders, *Swing Trading* bridges the gap between long-term "buy-&-holders" and day traders. Now, CNBC/MSN *Money's* Jon Markman presents the highly profitable, risk-abating benefits of Swing.

$29.95   *Item #T186X-821613*

The Dow Theory

by Robert Rhea

Published by Barron's in September 1932, this is an explanation of Dow Theory development and an attempt to define its usefulness as an aid to speculation. Rhea carefully studied 252 editorials of Dow and Hamilton in order to present Dow Theory in terms that would be useful for the individual investor.

$16.95   *Item #T186X-11265*

The 7 Chart Patterns that Consistently Make Money

by Ed Downs

Discover 7 chart patterns that are key predictors of direction in any market. Whether you're an active trader or occasional investor, if you confirm your entries with these simple patterns, you'll be light years ahead of the average investor.

$19.95   *Item #T186X-11559*

Encyclopedia of Chart Patterns

by Thomas Bulkowski

In addition to utilizing various indicators that help identify trends, there is a multitude of chart patterns in this new book that will tell the analyst whether the stock or commodity is in a bullish or bearish mode.

$79.95   *Item #T186X-10781*

Trading Classic Chart Patterns

by Thomas Bulkowski

In his follow-up to the well-received *Encyclopedia of Chart Patterns*, Thomas Bulkowski gives traders a practical game plan to capitalize on established chart patterns. Written for the novice investor but with techniques for the professional, *Trading Classic Chart Patterns* includes easy-to-use performance tables, vivid case studies, and a scoring system that makes trading chart patterns simple.

$69.95   Item #T186X-85081

Market Evaluation and Analysis for Swing Trading
by David S. Nassar and Bill Lupein

Nassar and Lupien, two of the industry's most influential traders, share with readers their techniques and strategies for successful swing trading in today's market. You'll learn how to work the market to your advantage by recognizing supply and demand imbalances, reading the strength of bids and offers, and spotting market maker trading patterns. This "must-have" guide is an essential resource for every swing trader.

$55.00   Item # T186X-1661626

Technical Analysis of the Financial Markets
by John Murphy

From how to read charts to understanding indicators and the crucial role of technical analysis in investing, you won't find a more thorough or up-to-date source. Revised and expanded for today's changing financial world, it applies to equities as well as the futures markets.

$70.00   Item # T186X-10239

Technical Analysis of Stock Trends, 8th edition
by W.H.C. Bassetti, Robert D. Edwards, and John Magee

The universally acclaimed investor's classic has now been updated with the latest data and references. With more than 800,000 copies in previous editions, this is the definitive reference on

analyzing trends in stock performance. It incorporates the most recent stock information and updated charts for expert guidance.
$109.95   *Item #T186X-17379*

EDUCATIONAL VIDEO COURSES

Swing Trading with Oliver Velez

Finally a video workshop on Swing Trading! Comes with online manual featuring everything you need to master Swing Trading and take it to new levels of success.
$99.00   *Item #T186X-11356*

Proven Chart Patterns: Key Indicators for Success in Today's Markets with Chris Manning

Master trader Chris Manning presents proven, reliable chart patterns that pinpoint buy/sell signals for short- and longer-term investors—plus precise indicators for developing each pattern. Manning's clear, comprehensive style is easy enough, even for those new to technical analysis.
$64.95   *Item #T186X-41588*

Winning Chart Patterns with Ed Downs

Pinpoint high probability trades over and over again, using 7 chart patterns that are consistent winners. This in-depth training course provides step-by-step instruction on how to analyze and identify patterns that produce dramatic profits—trade after trade.
$99.00   *Item #T186X-17332*

Own The Knowledge

Established by traders, for traders, MarketWise has made a name for themselves by providing quality education and guidance to help the serious trader & short term investor navigate any market.

COURSES INCLUDE:

- TradeWise - MarketWise Trading School's Direct Access Trading 5-Day Course
- WiseAnalysis - MarketWise Trading School's Advanced Technical Analysis 2-Day Course
- MarketWise/McMillan Options - MarketWise Trading School's Advanced Options 2-Day Course

STUDENTS LEARN FROM:

- Explanations of high probability setups
- Live trading in class
- Multiple instructors with years of experience
- Small classes and professional classrooms
- Hands-on training with real-time trading
- Money management techniques & psychology

MarketWise Trading School: Training and education continues after the class ends.

CONTINUE YOUR EDUCATION WITH:

- 2-week RealTick® trading simulator after the TradeWise course.
- Online mentoring through Wise-Ex; real-time trades and information via Web conferencing & WiseGuide providing market updates 5 times a day.
- One month FREE subscription to WiseGuide & Wise-Ex online services after the TradeWise Course.

Sign up now for a FREE, no obligation, live online event with a MarketWise instructor at:
www.marketwise.com or call 1-877-658-9473
Remember space is limited so sign up today.

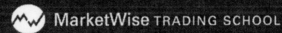 MarketWise TRADING SCHOOL

Free 2 Week Trial Offer for U.S. Residents From Investor's Business Daily:

INVESTOR'S BUSINESS DAILY will provide you with the facts, figures, and objective news analysis you need to succeed.

Investor's Business Daily is formatted for a quick and concise read to help you make informed and profitable decisions.

To take advantage of this free 2 week trial offer,
e-mail us at customerservice@traderslibrary.com
or visit our website at www.traderslibrary.com where
you find other free offers as well.

You can also reach us by calling 1-800-272-2855
or fax us at 410-964-0027.

About the Author

Michael C. Thomsett has written over 50 finance and investment books. He is the author of the successful *Getting Started in Options* (John Wiley & Sons) now in its fifth edition, which has sold over 175,000 copies. He also wrote *Investment and Securities Dictionary,* which was named by *Choice Magazine* an outstanding academic book of the year and was also published as a Webster's Dictionary. He also wrote *Master Fundamental Analysis* and *Mastering Technical Analysis* (Dearborn).

Thomsett also has written several real estate investment books, including *J. K. Lasser's Real Estate Investing* (John Wiley & Sons). He resides in Washington State and has been writing for 25 years.

About David S. Nassar

President and CEO of MarketWise Trading School, L.L.C. David S. Nassar is a pioneer in electronic trading. Seen on CNBC, NBC Nightly News, and CNN, and interviewed in numerous national publications including *The Wall Street Journal, BusinessWeek,* and *Forbes,* Nassar is the founder of a highly successful day trading school and the author of the book *Rules of the Trader,* and the NY Times bestseller, *How to Get Started in Electronic Day Trading.*

His vast market knowledge and continual trading experience has been transformed into courses, seminars, and books teaching the methods of an active trader. The rules and strategies developed by David are all incorporated in the MarketWise Methodology.

Printed in the United States
67163LVS00004B/38